Spilled Curry

To my Grandma Sophie & Uncle Mike

© 2019 Nick Rafter
ISBN 978-1-7340510-1-8

Spilled Curry

Nick Rafter

Table of Contents

Foreword 1

Chapter 1 - First Impressions 3

Chapter 2 - Move-In Day 15

Chapter 3 - Tears, Pills, and a Jar of Pickles 25

Chapter 4 - Chanisms 31

Chapter 5 - First Day of School 33

Chapter 6 - First Day of School: The Proposal 39

Chapter 7 - First Week of School: Awkward BBQ 43

Chapter 8 - Pissed Off 47

Chapter 9 - The Curry Incident of 2016 53

Chapter 10 - Soup for the Homeless 57

Chapter 11 - "I Think I'm Dying" 73

Chapter 12 - Chan, The Human E.M.P. 81

Chapter 13 - The Coffee Shack Girl Returns 95

Chapter 14 - The Beginning of the Second Semester 101

Chapter 15 - Our Trip to Ranch 99 111

Chapter 16 - SICK 117

Chapter 17 - Backdraft 125

Chapter 18 - Mama Chan 137

Chapter 19 - Presentations... 149

Chapter 20 - Chan Returns! From Spring Break................. 163

Chapter 21 - Crashing 181

Chapter 22 - Finals Week... 191

Chapter 23 - Night on the Town 209

Chapter 24 - Summer... 219

Chapter 25 - Fuckin' Chan, Man!.. 231

Chapter 26 - Spilled Curry 239

About the Author 251

Acknowledgements 252

Foreword

Hello, my name is Nick Rafter. What you are about to read is a collection of memorable moments from my time living with my two college roommates. One is my best friend, and the other is the most oblivious person in the world.

Okay, maybe that was a slight exaggeration. Not the whole world, but he is definitely the most oblivious person I have come to know. I don't mean to brag, but I have over three hundred and fifty friends on Facebook. So, I know nine real people. Out of the nine, he is just the worst. This individual lacks common sense, self-awareness, and a shirt that fits. Despite his lapses in character and fashion, he is a nice guy, which made living with him very difficult. I would've preferred if he was just a douche, but unfortunately, he was a douche with a heart, which made confronting him on certain issues very tough. This was because he was, as I mentioned earlier, so very unaware of when he was being a douche. Ugh, just thinking about it stresses me out. Writing this book is going to turn me into a day drinker.

One of the things you will pick up on while reading this book is that I am an asshole. But, with that said, so were my roommates. We were like a less glamorous Three Musketeers. The three A-holes! When you have an apartment with three assholes, everything inevitably turns to shit. Enjoy.

Chapter 1 - First Impressions

It was July 2015 when I met the fuck. I met him in a parking garage across from the entrance to San Jose State University. This meetup was organized by my best friend and my roommate from junior year, Alex. Alex is a short fellow with Facebook-logo blue eyes and un-styled, dirty-blonde hair. Alex somehow manages to look ten and fifty-five at the same time. He looks like a withered boy. He could pass as a child from the Industrial Revolution, or the Dust Bowl; he's like one of those kids that lived in a place where child labor laws weren't enforced. What Alex lacks in height, he more than compensates for with his outgoing personality and vast knowledge of sports. In fact, Alex is annoyingly knowledgeable—though just in sports, let's not get ahead of ourselves. Alex once asked me what opposable thumbs were during a game of Cards Against Humanity. During that same game, he asked me what a sorcerer was. Look, the kid is not joining MENSA any time soon. One of Alex's redeeming qualities, however, is his sense of humor. He's pretty funny, but don't tell him I told you that. I don't want to feed into his ego, which is located on the top floor of his Napoleon complex.

So, the meetup. I sat in the back seat of Alex's Subaru. Our mutual friend, Drew, sat up front. Drew is much taller than Alex and I at six-foot-two, which is six inches taller than me, and a foot taller than Alex. He has a slender physique, with longish golden hair. Picture Shaggy from *Scooby Doo*, just more of a pothead. Drew is one of those people that does not care what others' opinions of him are. You don't even have to know Drew to recognize this quality. You can tell just by looking at him. Drew always looks like he just got back from camping, tired and sunburnt—not to mention his attire. He often sports mismatched socks, worn out shoes, a shirt with at least three holes in it, and a backpack filled with unread textbooks and marijuana. I respect Drew's carefree attitude. He's like a yard sale: what you see is what you get. He keeps it real and never puts on a metaphorical mask. Drew's authenticity is admirable to me, as I am the opposite. I am shy, so I keep my thoughts and cynical remarks to myself. Alex, Drew, and I have been friends since high school, and that day, Drew was accompanying me and Alex on our apartment hunt.

While waiting in the back seat, I felt uneasy. I had mixed feelings about the meetup but realized it wasn't so much the meetup part that I was apprehensive about. It was really disdain for the whole concept of a third roommate. I was heavily against having a third roommate because (in my opinion) Alex and I had a good thing going. Adding a new variable could tarnish what I considered a good living situation. In addition to that, there would be no way to catch up a new roommate on all the arbitrary inside jokes we shared. Believe me, there was a lot. However, being broke college students, Alex and I did not have the luxury of acquiring a two-bedroom apartment in Silicon Valley without a third person. This meant a third roommate was inevitable. Which brings us to Chan, whom I eloquently described earlier as "the fuck."

While we were waiting for Chan to meet us in the parking garage across from the school, I decided to interrogate Alex about Chan. He was a completely unknown variable. I had to gather as much intel as I could before he arrived.

From the back seat, I asked, "So, Alex, how do you know Chan?"

Alex's response surprised me. He said that he didn't really know him, but he knew of him. *Great*, I thought, *a complete stranger*. My parents always warned me to stay away from them, and now I'm going to live with one? I suppose the term *stranger danger* loses its weight if the stranger helps with rent. I asked Alex how he knew of Chan. Chan happened to be Alex's dad's friend's client's son. Alex explained Chan was also starting school, and had been apartment hunting as well. It was at this moment I closed my eyes and made a wish. I wished to be wealthy, just so I could afford not to have a third roommate. I often daydream of scenarios where I am wealthy to avoid life's minor inconveniences. I remember daydreaming about having a penthouse in downtown San Jose. I had a great view of the city. *Ah, what a life!* I was obviously still so irked by the whole third-roommate idea, I had escaped to delusions of Gatsby-esque wealth.

After conducting my worthless interrogation with Alex, Chan finally pulled up. As I glanced out the passenger window, I got my first glimpse of Chan. He drove by us in a small, white, two-door Saab convertible. It was the type of car that your uncle's friend with the hair piece would drive. Chan was Asian, with a round face, not that the two were related. Just an observation. Once Chan had parked and got out of his car, I was able to fully see what we were dealing with. My eyes lit up. Chan was thought-provokingly huge. I wondered how someone so big could fit into a car so small. It was quite impressive. He towered over his petite vehicle. He was six-foot-five and a very solid 300lb. I felt bad, for his car; it must have been straining to lug him around everywhere. Chan was wearing a t-shirt that was a size too small and cargo shorts. I would soon learn this outfit was his signature look.

He entered Alex's car and sat in the back next to me. We exchanged pleasantries.

He extended his hand and said, "Hi, my name is Nick."

As I reached out to shake his hand, I sarcastically said, "Wow, great name, I love it. Nick is such a cool name. Oh, by the way, my name is also Nick."

Chan just stared at me, as if he was trying to figure out if I was joking or not.

"Two Nicks? That might get confusing living under one roof," said Alex, looking back at the two of us. I quickly and casually mentioned that I was born first, so I get priority. Nick Chan said that we could just call him by his last name, Chan. This was the day Chan was born. This was what Victor

Frankenstein must have felt when he reanimated a sampler platter of human body parts. We had, indeed, created a monster, or at least agreed to live with one.

Once introductions were out of the way, we set off on our apartment hunt. During our time in the car with Chan, I tried to observe him and attempt to get a read on him. In the car, Chan called various homeowners and property managers to try and book appointments to view apartments. He was fearless, and I admired that. I, on the contrary, have a lot of social anxiety and find it excruciating to talk on the phone with strangers. I took note of his presumed social skills. In my mind, I was thinking, *He seems normal*. There were no red flags. Ugh, why weren't there any red flags?!

Finally, after an hour of sitting in a hot, cramped car with Alex, Drew, and Chan, we got an appointment to tour an apartment complex located on the other side of town. On our way to the apartment complex, I quickly realized that this place would be a no-go. We had been driving a while. The location seemed to be further from the school than where I would like to be. Ideally, I would want to live no further than a mile from the school. This is because my bike is my primary source of transportation, and the heat in San Jose is an unfortunate variable that one must consider when riding a bike. I really did not want to show up sweaty to school every day, thus living in a one-mile radius of the campus was ideal.

This apartment was about three miles north of the school. I told the guys the place was too far.

Chan said something along the lines of, "I don't mind the distance."

Ah, Chan, Chan, Chan...so naive. The San Jose sun can be a real ultraviolet bitch. It's wasn't his fault, he didn't know any better. You see, this was Chan's first year at college away from home. I looked at Alex, and I could tell he wasn't thrilled with the location either. It was far, and we had to go through a somewhat questionable neighborhood. But we had an appointment, and we decided we might as well check it out. After all, it was also our only appointment...

After navigating through the sketchy neighborhood, we pulled up to a surprisingly nice-looking leasing office. I imagine this is what it's like to stumble upon USC. After we parked, we flocked to the front door like children on Halloween. Unfortunately, we were greeted by a sign on the door that read, "Leasing office is closed for renovation. Please follow the trail of red arrow-shaped signs to get to the leasing office." My initial distaste for this place was reinforced by the use of the *Comic Sans* font. This place instantly lost all credibility. I mean, use a font with a little more authority, like **Impact**, or Verdana. We followed the red arrow signs for what felt like an eternity. We turned left, then right, left, then right, weaving through various hallways. Finally, we came across an apartment unit with a handwritten sign taped to the door: leasing office.

After knocking on the door, we were greeted by a polite young Indian man. I don't remember his name, but for the sake of the story, I'm going to refer to him as "Raj." Raj welcomed us into the office and told us to have a seat at his desk. As we walked in, my eyes naturally darted around the room. His "office" was pretty much shit. I mean, it wasn't even an office. It was a one-bedroom apartment with a desk in the living room. Alex and Chan sat at his desk while Drew and I pulled up some chairs. Raj asked what we were looking for. Alex explained that we were looking for a three-bedroom, two-bath apartment. Raj nodded his head and started typing on his computer.

We sat quietly while Raj clicked away at his keyboard. We endured this awkward silence for about five minutes. During this time, I scanned the room to get an indication of the unit because this "office" was an apartment, after all. The room was pretty dim, with zero natural light. It was illuminated by a single fluorescent light in the kitchen. All the fixtures and cabinets were cheap looking. *You couldn't pay me to stay here*, I thought. *A little commercial art would go a long way. It would definitely distract you from the eyesore that is the kitchen. Laminate countertops? Gross. No stainless steel? I can't. Pressboard cabinets? I won't. What's the hold up, Raj? How long does it take to check the availability of an apartment? God, this room is dark and depressing. This place is where dreams go to die. I don't want to be here, let alone live here. I have been in here five minutes and I have already developed a vitamin D deficiency. Why is he clicking so vigorously? He is probably finishing up a game of Minesweeper. Do people still play that? Ah, who am I kidding? Raj is definitely a Minesweeper guy.*

My rambling thoughts were interrupted.

"Sorry for the delay," apologized Raj.

He told us that he wasn't the leasing agent there. He actually worked in another complex and was just there filling in, and was not used to the computer. *We all know you were sweeping those mines*, I thought. Raj informed us that there were no three-bedroom apartments available, but he did have a two-bedroom that we could tour. I made a face. I couldn't help it. This whole day had been a waste of time. Raj said that if we wanted, we could transfer units when a three-bedroom unit became available. I already knew this was not going to happen, but I could tell Chan wanted to see the apartment. I will admit that I was curious to see the apartment, too. It had to be better than the leasing office, right? It wasn't.

We followed Raj through the maze that was the apartment complex. We then went up three flights of stairs to the apartment. During our trek up the stairs, I was picturing carrying furniture. It was an uncomfortable thought, but only for a moment, as I knew this thought wasn't going to be a reality. After checking out the depressing two bedrooms, we ventured back to the apartment—I mean, leasing office. You know what I mean.

During our walk back, an unprovoked Raj struck up a conversation with me.

Raj questioned me about my education. "Where do you go to college?" "What's your major?" What is this...an interview?

I told him I was senior at SJSU and that I was majoring in creative arts. Since I was a student, people often asked me about school, and when I would tell them I was a senior, they'd have an impressed look on their face. But, when I mentioned to them I was a creative arts major, their faces would lose any evidence of being impressed. They completely lost interest. I'm assuming they thought I was finger painting and making macaroni sculptures all day. To avoid looking any ruder, they would give a generic response like, "Oh, that's nice," or, "That seems cool."

After immediately losing interest in my schooling, Raj proceeded to tell me his aspirations of transferring into UC Berkeley. What a jerk. How dare he try to one-up me by saying he wants to go to a more prestigious school? *What's this guy's fucking deal?* Clearly, I had a lot of natural resentment toward Raj. Not only did he plan on going to a better school than I, but he had a job. I was unemployed at the time and felt somewhat lesser for not being as successful as the nice leasing agent. I felt a lot of anxiety toward my future. Will I be able to find work once I graduate? Will I graduate? These questions always rose to my mind when I met someone my age already gainfully employed.

Once we returned to the leasing office, Alex and I did all the talking. We acted like we might be interested, when in reality, it was never going to happen. Poor Chan had no idea of our intentions.

Once we were in the car, I said, "Well, that place is a no."

"Definitely!" exclaimed Alex.

Chan looked surprised. He seemed somewhat clueless as to why we had ill will for this place. Here's the thing, Alex and I were somewhat spoiled when it came to apartments. We stayed at an exceptional apartment complex during our junior year. We told Chan about the place, and about how great it was. Then it hit us. Why don't we see if they have a unit available? Yeah, I know, we're idiots.

So, we drove down to the new complex, called "La Playa." We parked the car and walked down a pathway with a pool located to the left and another to the right. Yup, that's right, two pools! Directly at the end of the pathway was a large leasing office. The lobby of the leasing office was very hip looking. The walls were decorated with replica Banksy paintings, and on every flat surface was a chrome-coated sculpture. The only songs they played were Taylor Swift and Katy Perry. We were greeted by a leasing agent named Janet. Janet was a very friendly white woman with short, reddish hair. She had an Emma Stone vibe. Very cool. Alex and I explained to her that we were looking for a three-bedroom unit. She scanned her computer screen for a moment and then told us, "Sorry, guys, we don't have any three-bedrooms available, but there is a two-bedroom available."

Chan looked interested and I, despite my contempt for the two-bedroom idea, was actually okay with it, but only because we had a similar unit the year before. The location of La Playa was also a ten-minute bike ride from school. I asked Janet for an application. She said that we could fill out the applications online, so we exited the leasing office. On our way back to return Chan to his petite convertible in the parking garage, we discussed the living situation. Chan wanted to get a place ASAP. He said he would sleep anywhere, he just wanted to get in a place so there was one less thing to worry about before starting college. This, I found completely understandable, especially being someone with a lot of anxiety. Having one less thing to worry about is always a good thing.

We all agreed to apply online for the apartment. The two-bedroom apartment we applied for was more like a townhouse. The first floor had a decent-sized living room, a kitchen, and a bathroom, which was connected to a bedroom. On the second floor was a decent-sized loft overlooking the living room. Next to the loft was the master bedroom. The master bedroom had a huge walk in closet, along with its own bathroom.

The arrangement we came up with in the car was that Alex and I would get the bedrooms and Chan would get the loft. Alex and I would have to pay a bigger portion of rent, but that's cool. We were all in agreement. By the time we got back to the parking garage, we were all excited and relieved about our new living situation. I remember Chan inquiring about the living situation, asking simple things like:

"Do you guys have any rules?"

I quickly said, "Oh, we don't need to talk about that now."

Chan said, "Okay, let's just not be assholes."

Oh, how I wish he took his own advice.

We were all in good spirits and ready for this new chapter of our lives. I remember feeling very optimistic. After Chan returned to his car and we embarked on our return home, I said, "I think this is going to work out." Boy, was I wrong.

Chapter 2 - Move-In Day

Three weeks had passed since our visit to the La Playa leasing office. I was up early, lounging at my mom's townhouse and drinking coffee, waiting for Alex to pick me up with the U-Haul. As I sipped my piping-hot cup of coffee, I went over my list of things to pack into the U-Haul; I didn't want to forget anything. My phone started to ring.

It was Alex. "Hey are you on the way?" I asked.

"No, I'm here," said Alex.

"Here, as in close by?"

"No, I'm here, as in, in front of your garage."

"Oh, I guess I'll be right out." I had thought he would call me to tell me he was on the way, so I chugged my hot cup of coffee and ran down to the garage to start moving my stuff into the U-Haul.

We spent about twenty minutes loading the U-Haul with my stuff, which is a pretty good time, not that anyone was keeping track. Well, I guess I was. This was my second time moving from home to be closer to school, so I had some experience with packing. My first time moving away, I made the mistake of bringing too much stuff. This time around, I only brought the essentials: clothes, desk, computer, printer, toothbrush, TV, and two Xboxes.

We then set off for a one-hour drive to San Jose. I'll admit that I was feeling anxious toward the drive, but this is a familiar feeling; I feel anxiety before any car ride. I was especially wary because Alex was driving a large truck, and the dimensions of the truck were bigger than his Subaru Impreza. I was nervous about being in a U-Haul with an amateur truck driver. But, once Alex and I started chatting about the upcoming school year, I began to get excited—not sexually. I was just very much looking forward to my last year of college. After a few minutes, my nerves settled, and I was ready for this new experience.

As we pulled up to La Playa, we passed by Chan sitting in his car. Alex and I got out of the U-Haul and approached Chan's tiny car. Chan got out and we all said our hellos. I asked Chan where his stuff was. His car was empty and today was move-in day.

"My dad is going to help me move in a couple of days," answered Chan.

Alex and Chan started to unload the U-Haul. Meanwhile, I went to the leasing office to drop off the deposit (which I fronted) and pick up the keys. I strolled into the hip leasing office and handed Janet the deposit. She played around on her computer for a couple of minutes and then handed me the keys.

"You're all set!"

I exited the leasing office with excitement. I may or may not have been skipping. I was hit with emotion. I felt like a real adult. Moving into a new apartment, starting a new chapter of my life. This jubilant wave of emotion crashed by the time I returned to the moving truck, due to the fact that I was about to spend all day moving. Like most people, I hate moving. In fact, does anybody like moving? If so, email me here: SpilledCurry@gmail.com. I don't even think professional movers like moving.

Before we began unloading the U-Haul, we all went to tour the new apartment. Alex and I already knew what it would look like, since we had a similar unit last year. In fact, we were in the same building as before. Our two-story apartment was fully carpeted except in the hallways, bathrooms, kitchen, and loft. It was newly renovated, so we had a very stylish-looking kitchen. Granite countertops and stainless steel appliances. Unfortunately, we had a very small kitchen, which Chan seemed to feel discontent with. The kitchen was about the size of Chan's car.

Alex and I didn't mind the small kitchen. Why would Chan not like the sparkly new kitchen? This apartment was much nicer and bigger than most college students have. So why complain? Yeah, the kitchen was small, but beggars can't be choosers. Let me repeat myself: STAINLESS STEEL. After noticing our puzzled faces, Chan informed us of his love of cooking. He then went on for a few minutes humble-bragging about how good he was at cooking. I say "humble-brag" because he would brag in the form of an offer.

"I can teach you how to cook this." "I can teach how to cook that." We'll get more into that later.

Chan was very helpful with the moving process. Since he was moving in a couple days later, he helped Alex and me with our stuff. This was the day where we not only learned of his talent for cooking but also of his strength. Chan was really strong. He just held out his arms and had Alex and I pile things on them. After we gave him the stuff to carry, he would say things like, "You guys can add more." He was our Chinese Hulk, which was a pretty accurate description. I mean, he was carrying an enormous amount of stuff while his body was desperately trying to escape his poor-fitting clothes. His strength was amazing. He could probably bench his petite car.

Alex and I were not the only ones to witness Chan's brute strength. Drew came by to help us move. He was also impressed with Chan's strength. Drew moved some of his things into the apartment as well. He was going to stay with us for a couple weeks until he could find a place of his own. Drew brought a dresser full of clothes, a couple pairs of shoes, and of course, some pot. We spent the rest of the day carrying things from the U-Haul to the apartment.

It was a beautiful Saturday afternoon in Silicon Valley. A week had passed since Alex and I moved into the apartment. Alex was watching TV downstairs with Drew. I was upstairs browsing Amazon for ethernet cables. Alex and I had spent the week negotiating with the cable company and setting up an account with our local power company. Alex was able to get a great deal on cable and internet, and we were spending our Saturday enjoying it. I was browsing ethernet cables because I wanted the best internet possible. I like to play video games. Having a great internet connection is pretty paramount.

I spent hours in my room upstairs browsing Amazon for ethernet cables. I read the reviews, compared prices, and looked at photos. I do an immense amount of research before any purchase. This is because I'm indecisive to a fault. Also, I want the best quality for my buck.

I was startled when the front door burst open, banging the wall behind it. I heard Alex and Drew say, "Hey, Chan." I then heard some unfamiliar voices, but they were too faint to make out. A few moments later, I turned around to see Chan, his dad, and his younger brother. My room door opens into the loft that would become Chan's room. At the time of Chan's intrusion, my door was open. Chan introduced us to his family. His dad and brother looked fairly similar. I was amused that all three of them wore cargo shorts. Alex, Drew, and I offered to help Chan move. After all, it was the least we could do. Chan was generous enough to help us move in, so it was only right that we extend him the same courtesy.

Chan moved in various items, like his desk, clothes, a plant, cooking supplies, a bed, a wooden cupboard with a broken door, and one hideously floral-patterned loveseat. The loveseat looked like something that came from his grandma's house. We were all standing in Chan's room to catch our breath when I broke the silence and said, "Hey, nice couch, Chan."

"Thanks, my grandma gave it to me," said Chan.

Whelp, that explains that. Now that Chan's stuff was moved in, it was time to assemble furniture. Nothing is more uncomfortable than listening to three people argue about building furniture. Alex and Drew were downstairs resuming their TV show and I was upstairs adding things to my cart. We were all forced to listen to Chan and his father argue about building a computer chair. The arguments were formulated like this:

"I think this goes here."

"No, that goes there!"

Then Chan's little brother would chime in with, "When are we going home?"

Chan and his father would simultaneously respond with, "SHUT UP!"

This went on for forty long, excruciating minutes. It was uncomfortably awkward, like getting an erection in church. This palpable feeling would soon become the norm for anything involving Chan.

After the Chans finished building the chair, there was some shuffling around. I was in the middle of thanking the Lord for ending the arguing when I was interrupted by more arguing. They had begun building Chan's desk. Why I had to endure this, I will never know. Fortunately, like most iPhone owners, my phone came with headphones. These were put to use blocking out the Chans and their irritating bickering. The arguing seemed to stop and resume in waves. Stop and go, on again, off again, just like Katy Perry and John Mayer.

Speaking of John Mayer, I was listening to some Taylor Swift, when I heard a knock at the door. I turned around and saw Chan and his father standing in the doorway. I pulled my headphones out, and like Kanye, Chan interrupted Taylor.

"Hey, do you know where the modem is?" asked Chan.

Chan's father was trying to connect Chan's computer to the internet. I told them that the modem was downstairs. Chan's dad was inquiring about the ethernet port. The only activated port was downstairs and in use with the modem. I said that if he wanted, he could purchase a splitter and have one cord go from the splitter to Chan's computer and the other into the modem. Why he didn't want to just have the cord from the modem to his computer is beyond me.

Chan's dad told me that splitters for ethernet don't exist. He went on to tell me that you can't split a signal. He was right about the signal but wrong about the splitters. You can get them on Amazon.com for $8.98.

"Good thing you have a background in I.T., Dad!" blurted Chan's brother.

Thanks for the info that no one asked for, I thought. Chan's brother said that to try and impress me. I wasn't amused, or impressed. I was annoyed at Chan's brother's attempt to build up his father in front of me. Chan's dad asked about my internet. I told him that I was using the Wi-Fi, but I planned on getting a long ethernet cord to connect the modem to my computer. As I spoke, Chan's dad's mouth was slightly agape. I found it very distracting.

I also mentioned that I was actually about to order a cord on Amazon that day.

In an authoritative tone, Chan's dad said, "Don't do that, I'm going down to Computer City to pick some things up for Nick; I'll grab you a cord."

"Oh, wow. Thank you," I said. Maybe enduring the argument was worth it? *I just saved seven dollars*, I thought. So, the Chans took off to Computer City, thus reinstating the peaceful atmosphere that they had polluted with their constant arguing.

During our well-deserved break from the Chans, Alex and Drew were able to watch their show. I was in my room, back on my computer. I removed the ethernet cord from my Amazon list. If you haven't noticed by now, I'm a stereotypical millennial who relies all too much on technology. I enjoy the convenience of being able to shop online, plus getting to avoid small talk with a nosey cashier who keeps asking me about the items I'm purchasing. Personally, I view Amazon as a godsend, same with Netflix, and boxed wine. These things make life good. Peace was restored to the apartment and everyone lived happily ever after. "Ever after" lasted about one hour and twenty minutes.

Chan and his family returned to the apartment. I could tell it was them by the sound our door made when it was flung open. I was on my computer, getting my Amazon fix, when I heard a knock at my door. It was Chan, and he let me know that he, his father, and his garbage pail brother had returned from Computer City and had my cord. At that moment, Chan's dad made his way into the loft, aka Chan's room. Chan's dad handed me the ethernet cord.

"That'll be twenty-five bucks," said Chan's dad.

I threw up a little bit in my mouth. Twenty-five dollars for a cord?! The same exact cord I was going to buy online for seven dollars? I made a face. It was the type of face you make when you're dissatisfied with something but have to pretend everything is fine. You know the face you make when your parents get you a gift that indicates that they know nothing about you or your interests? Mom.

I became conscious that I was making this face, so I forced a smile to try to make things better. It's very difficult to smile when you really don't want to. In fact, I didn't smile, I just flashed him my upper teeth and nodded my head. To make matters worse, as a result of my internal battle, a vein started bulging from my forehead. This is the vein that only appears when you're at the gym working out, or in the bathroom pushing something out.

Despite my poor physical state, I managed to say, "Thanks! Can I give Chan the money to pass on to you? I don't have any cash on me."

"Yup, that's fine," said Chan's dad.

I went to my room to quietly scream into a pillow. I felt swindled. The way Chan's father had phrased that he was getting the cord made it seem as if it was being gifted. I went from thinking I was saving seven dollars to losing twenty-five.

Now I had to pay twenty-five dollars for a cord because Chan's father didn't know how to bargain shop. I know freaking out over twenty-five dollars may seem somewhat extreme, but twenty-five dollars can go a long way for a broke college student. Just think of all the Top Ramen you can buy for twenty-five dollars! I could have used that money on notebooks, groceries, or more realistically, some drinks that I so desperately needed after this ordeal.

Chapter 3 - Tears, Pills, and a Jar of Pickles

It was the week before school, and I had just arrived at the apartment. After moving day, I spent what was left of summer back home with my family. As I was walking up the steps to my apartment, I could hear our TV. I wondered who it could be; I knew Alex wasn't moving in until Sunday, and today was Thursday. As I got closer to the door, I started to make out the sound from the TV. It was the news. At this point, Alex was definitely not the culprit. This left Chan. I opened the door, and sure enough, there he was sitting on the couch. We made the nice and said our hellos. I asked him when he had officially moved in and started living there. He told me that he had been there since Monday. I asked him how he was doing living on his own for the first time.

Without taking his eyes off the screen, he casually said, "I have been crying the past couple days. It's been a hard transition."

I had been in the apartment less than a minute and things were already weird. Since Chan's family only lived thirty minutes away, I suggested that it might be a good idea for him to visit his family on the weekends, thus weaning him into independence. He slowly nodded his head up and down while staring at the TV screen. I just stood there feeling like The Clash, unsure if I should stay or go. After a few awkward seconds, I came to the conclusion that I should quickly get out of there. Plus, watching an adult man sob and watch the news wasn't what I wanted to do with my day.

I spent most of the day doing what I do best: binging shows on Netflix. I was about halfway through the last season of *30 Rock* when I was interrupted by a faint noise. At first, I ignored the noise, hoping it would make like a magician's assistant and disappear. The faint noise didn't go away, and it was all I could focus on while watching my show. Eventually, I couldn't take the subtle yet increasingly annoying noise anymore. Now I had to pause my episode and investigate. Where was the noise coming from? I got up and moved silently to my door. With each step, the noise got louder and louder. Right when I got up to my door, I was almost able to make out the sound. It sounded like a little girl whimpering. Kind of like the ghost girl, Moaning Myrtle, from the *Harry Potter* series. I put my ear to the door. Unfortunately, the noise was not a moaning ghost; the noise was Chan, sobbing in front of his computer. The poor guy was homesick, and I felt bad for him.

Again, I found myself questioning what I should do, if anything. As I stood in front of the door contemplating, Chan was on the phone, breaking down to his mom, so, naturally, I stood with my ear pressed against the door, eavesdropping. If I were to do something, I would have to wait until he got off the phone. As I listened in, I could hear him telling his mom that he missed her and that living alone was hard. While he was crying, I realized that if his mom couldn't cheer him up, then the odds of me cheering him up weren't in my favor. So, I did what any kind-hearted person would do: I went back to watching *30 Rock*. I couldn't have Chan's sobbing interrupt Liz Lemon every five seconds, so I put some headphones on and turned up the volume.

A couple hours later, unbeknownst to me, Chan had invited some friends over. Not that it was a big deal—I just would have liked a courtesy heads-up that people were coming over. They stayed downstairs in the living room and watched *Family Guy*. The walls in our apartment were pretty thin; I could hear the theme song (I sang along, of course). I could also hear bits and pieces of the conversations they were having. I heard a girl's voice ask Chan how living away from home was going. He told her that it was going pretty well. It seemed like a bit of an overstatement, considering Chan spent the day crying. I was not in the mood to make the nice and socialize, so I skipped dinner and stayed in my room. Luckily, I had a box of Fiber One bars to snack on. The only negative about snacking on a box of Fiber One bars is the aftermath that hits in the morning. Luckily, we had a Costco card and bought toilet paper in bulk.

I know not eating dinner to avoid socializing is a bit neurotic. I completely get that, but I was not in the mood to socialize. I'm rarely in the mood to socialize. I grew up in a small town, and if I am on Park Street (our poorly named main street), I'm bound to see someone I recognize. I actively try to avoid that street, but on the off chance that I'm on that street and I see someone I know, I go out of my way to avoid a stop and chat. I'm pretty good at spotting people, so I can usually maneuver across the street before I'm recognized. If I can't do that, then I can quickly shuffle into a little shop and wait for them to go by. So, I had no problem hiding up in my room.

As I watched some more Netflix and snacked on some Fiber One bars, I began to notice a smell. It smelled like burning broccoli. Yes, I know what burning broccoli smells like, and yes, I can't cook. Get over it. I began to sniff around my room and investigate. Then I noticed the smell wafting in through the vent. The other end of the vent was near the kitchen, so I began to think maybe Chan had burnt something while cooking. I started to hear muffled voices echoing from the vent, leading me to put my ear on the vent and listen. I could hear them talking about vaping.

Ugh, vaping. Chan was a vapor-er...vaporist? Anyway, he was smoking pot in a vape machine. And all the vapor was being sucked into my room. Honestly, what's the deal with vaping? If you're going to smoke, then smoke. Don't *kinda* do it. It's like competing in a BMX event at the X-Games with training wheels on. It's not as cool or as dangerous as the real thing. His friends eventually left, and I was able to get some sleep (or so I thought).

I was awakened in a manner which no man should experience. I woke up to Chan crying on the phone to his mom. Again, with this guy? I was lying down, looking up at the ceiling fan that I had left on all night. I couldn't fall back asleep, so I just laid there, listening to him sob. I began to wonder if this living situation was a bad idea. Was it going to be like this every morning? After about eight minutes, the crying stopped. I heard some shuffling around. I then heard the door slam shut. If the crying doesn't wake you, the door slamming sure will.

Chan had left to visit home. I was annoyed. How can someone have such bad door etiquette? I enjoyed my Friday. I watched TV in the living room and sipped coffee. As I watched the TV, I began to feel strange. I could feel my face numb and the back of my head tingle with a burning sensation. *Is this a stroke?* I thought. I then felt a strong emotional wave of guilt. After about an hour of not being able to focus on anything, I, like Chan, called my mom. Without the waterworks, of course, because I'm an adult man. She dropped whatever plans she had and came down to visit. It was nice, but I still felt weird. We made an appointment to get checked out the next morning. After a couple hours hanging out with my ma, we went back home.

I woke up feeling worse. Luckily for me, my appointment was in a few hours. I met with my doctor and he asked about the numbness in my face. He asked if I had recently hit my head. I told him that the numbness had passed. He then asked if I was going through any life-changing events. I realized that maybe I had some anxiety about my last year in college. I wasn't nervous about college itself; I was more focused on life after college. Will I be able to get a job? Will I be able to work somewhere? Can I enjoy the work that I do and also get paid well? All these little things had built up and led to a minor panic attack. The doctor prescribed me some meds. After about three days of taking the medication, I felt great. I was back to normal, leading me to stop taking the medication. My dad called me for weeks afterward, asking if I had stopped taking the medication, because he was worried that I might get addicted. I don't have the attention span to get addicted to anything.

On Sunday, Alex showed up. We hung out and watched some sports. Chan soon showed up as well. The front door burst open and Chan appeared in the doorway with a giant jar of pickles. Again, with the door? I thought, *Is he just walking through life, slamming doors open and shut?* This jar of pickles would be the first of many items that Chan brought into our apartment that would never be used. It would be an item with no purpose other than taking up space.

Chapter 4 - Chanisms

During the first couple weeks of school, I started to notice some of Chan's "Chanisms." A Chanism is what Alex, Drew, and I referred to as one of Chan's annoying traits. For example, his inability to gently open and close a door. I started to pick up on some new Chanisms that I hadn't noticed before living with Chan. What I didn't realize at the time was that these quirks started to out-shine what I thought was his personality. Reflecting back now, I think these quirks weren't quirks at all. They were just personality traits of his that I didn't notice before living with him. You don't truly know someone until you live with them. I'm pretty sure Gandhi said that. The next couple chapters will cover some notable Chanisms that I observed during my first week living with him.

Chapter 5 - First Day of School

During the first week of residency with Chan, I started to notice these quirks. It was the morning of my first day of senior year. I was asleep in my bed when I was suddenly awoken by violent coughing. As I noted before, the walls of our apartment were paper thin, so when Chan coughed, it sounded like he was in the room, coughing directly into your ear. This went on for about twenty minutes. Unfortunately for me and Alex, this is how we would be woken up most days. I was now #woke two hours earlier than I would have liked, so I took a shower and got dressed. This took some time, since it was the first day of school and first impressions are everything. After trying on five different outfits, I decided on outfit number three.

I opened my door and tiptoed through Chan's loft. As I walked on eggshells, I glanced over to him. He was asleep on his bed in a pair of boxer briefs and his body was spread out. He looked like a sea creature that had washed up on the shore. Poor guy tuckered himself out with all that coughing. I made my way downstairs and made myself some coffee. While I waited for the coffee to brew, I went into Alex's room. His room door was cracked open and I could hear him listening to music. He too had been awoken by Chan's coughing. We both had a laugh about it, thinking it was a one-time occurrence. Little did we know, this would become part of our morning routine. After drinking my coffee and chatting with Alex, I left for school an hour early. That way, I had enough time to get another coffee and get a good seat in class.

I grabbed my bike and rode to school. Our apartment building was a straight shot to school. It was very convenient, and seemingly an easy ride. This was the same road I used to take to school the year before, and it made me feel nostalgic. It brought back many fond memories. I had been on this road hundreds of times, in the morning, afternoon, and night. It had been a long while since I had been on a bike and it showed; I was getting very tired, very quickly. *I didn't think I would be this out of shape*, I thought. About halfway to school, I realized that my tires were not fully pumped up, resulting in me putting a lot of effort into pedaling. I probably should have checked the tires before I started riding. Not only was the air in my tires out, the sun was out too. By the time I got to school, I was uncomfortably sweaty. I don't mind a sexy glisten, but I felt gross. The San Jose sun can be very unforgiving. My route has little to no shade. The sun is on you the whole time. Not to mention that the ride to school also has many stop signs, so stopping and then going every block with flat tires gets pretty tiring. I arrived at school sweaty and exhausted.

When I got to the campus, I jumped off my bike and walked it. I couldn't have anyone see me riding around with flat tires like an idiot. I quickly locked my bike in front the building where my class was being held. I then ran into the bathroom to clean up. I looked in the bathroom mirror to see the damage. It wasn't pretty. So much for first impressions. My hair was messed up and I was covered in sweat. I was a real hot mess. I grabbed some paper towels and dabbed my face with them. I grabbed some more paper towels and dabbed my armpits. These were desperate times. Which, as you know, call for desperate measures. So, I was practically bathing in the sink. I remember someone telling me that body odor was caused by bacteria, so I pressed soap into my hand and then rubbed the soap on my armpits. My string of logic at the time was that if I kill the bacteria with soap, there will be no odor. I then brushed my dark brown hair with water. I didn't look great, but I was able to smooth enough rough edges out to have a decent appearance. Give me a break, I was trying to look good on the first day. What if there was a pretty girl in my class? What if my future wife was in one of my classes? Spoiler alert: Nope, she wasn't.

With the remaining time I had after putting soap in my armpits, I went and grabbed some coffee. My class was on alternative cinema, and for some reason, it was being held in the business building, which was in a part of the campus I hadn't explored. I am a Creative Arts major. Most of my classes are in the same building. I had been to the business building once or twice last year to meet up with Alex. I remembered that there was a quaint little coffee shack next to the business building. I usually got coffee from the food court area of campus, so I was eager to try this place. I walked up to the counter and that's when I noticed her.

Last year, I used to have to walk back and forth from one end of campus to the other. I had classes that were one after the other, but they were on opposite sides of campus (enroll in classes asap, otherwise you end up in my situation). So, walking back and forth, you start to recognize people due to you passing by them every day. I used to walk past this cute brunette girl with enchanting eyes. She would always pass by me listening to her iPod. I would do the same. Anyway, said girl worked at this coffee shack.

I pretended to look at the menu to stall until I could figure out what to say. After all, this was my chance to talk to her, and first impressions are everything. I walked up to the counter, looked into her magical eyes, and said, "GIVE ME COFFEE, BETCH!"

Just kidding. That didn't happen. I'm just making sure you're still with me. I approached the counter feeling confident.

She asked me, "What can I get you?"

Her voice was soft and beautiful, and her eyes, her eyes…*Oh no! I forgot what I was going to say. Shoot! What was I going to say? Did she say something? What did she say? I thought I heard something. Her mouth definitely moved. C'mon, man, get it together.* I just stood there, frozen, for what felt like an eternity while my mind was in utter chaos. In reality, I was standing there looking at her for a couple of seconds. As my brain finished rebooting, I was able to start thinking logically.

She probably asked if I wanted to buy something. It's amazing to me that particular circumstances can make seconds feel like hours. *Say something, Nick, say something!*

"Uhhhh, I will havvvve theeeee cofffffeeee, please." (Probably the most unattractive way to talk to someone.)

While she got the coffee, I gave myself an internal pep talk. *Come on, Nick, you gotta save this thing.*

"Do you want room for cream?" she asked.

"Yes, please. Thanks!" *There you go, Nick, more of that.* As she returned with my coffee, I realized that I had to keep the conversation going.

"Will that be all?" she asked.

Now was my chance to converse a little more. "Are those muffins gluten free?" I asked, pointing to a plastic case on the counter which contained baked goods. Keep in mind, I'm not gluten-free; I just like knowing that I have the option. Anyway, I ended up with coffee and a gluten-free muffin. This would be the first of two awkward moments with the girl who worked at the coffee shack.

Chapter 6 - First Day of School: The Proposal

After class, I returned home to an empty apartment. While I waited for Alex, Drew, and Chan to return from class, I went on my favorite website, Amazon, to order some books. The guys showed up about an hour later. At this point, we were hungry. I went to go get some food out of the fridge. It was empty. That's right, we hadn't gone to the grocery store yet. Being young men with big appetites, we made going to the grocery store priority number one. We stopped what we were doing and immediately piled into Alex's car and set off to Trader Joe's. Chan and I sat in the back, while Alex and Drew sat up front. Chan had a look of excitement on his face. He found this moment to be the opportune time to propose an idea. He asked me and Alex if he could not pay for groceries, and in return, he would cook the food. The car got quiet. *Is this guy serious?* I thought.

"I'd rather you just split the cost of groceries and I'll cook my own food," I said, shutting down Chan's proposal.

He didn't say anything the rest of the way to the grocery store. I think he was genuinely shocked that we hadn't taken him up on his offer. The thing you need to know about Chan is that he is a really good cook. So good, in fact, that he works part-time as a personal chef. I think, by us not accepting his offer, he was personally taken aback. Later on, in the grocery store, Chan made another attempt at his proposal, putting me and Alex in an awkward situation. I told him we wanted to have him as a roommate, not a personal chef. I think he was able to understand where we were coming from. Alex and I were broke college kids, and a personal chef wasn't in the budget. He had a quizzical look but kept quiet. I could tell he was still bummed that we wanted no part of his proposal.

When we got home, he started cooking his own dinner while Alex and I went to the basketball court located in our apartment complex. Drew joined us in shooting some hoops.

While we were shooting, I said to the guys, "So, today in the car...That was strange, right?"

"What in the car?" asked Alex.

I gave Alex a look. "You know, when he proposed that absurd deal about the groceries?" I said.

"Oh, yeah, that was awkward," said Alex.

I took a shot and air balled, and as I went to retrieve the ball, I said, "I feel bad that he took it personally, but he has to understand that we agreed to room with a roommate, and a personal chef is not what we signed up for."

We returned back to the apartment and Chan had just finished cooking his dinner. Alex, Drew, and I began to brainstorm what to cook for our dinner. Honestly, we brainstormed what Alex was going to cook for dinner. Alex was the best cook out of the three of us. If I were to rank us, it would go: Alex, Drew, and then myself. But I'm always willing to help Alex out with prep work if he needs it. Once we decided that baked chicken was what we were having, Chan made a comment about how he was surprised that we don't really cook.

"It's so easy," he said.

Not everyone knows how to cook, I thought. He went on and on about all the things he knows how to cook. To be honest, the only person he was impressing was himself. Alex, Drew, and I all kind of nodded our heads with little to no enthusiasm. He then tried to make all his bragging sound less pretentious by saying, "If you guys ever need to know how to make something, feel free to ask me."

Now was my chance to strike, my chance to stump him. I wanted to ask him something that he didn't know how to make, and then it hit me.

"So, Chan, I have a cooking question," I said.

"What's up?" Chan answered.

"How does one unscramble an egg?" I asked.

"What?" responded Chan with a blank stare.

I repeated my question, "How does one unscramble an egg?"

"But...why? How?" said a perplexed Chan, trying to formulate a response.

"Let's say I was scrambling eggs and then realized I didn't want them scrambled."

"Well, I don't know, but I prefer poached eggs anyway. I'm really good at that."

"Oh, okay. Gotcha," I said. "But can you un-poach an egg?"

"Why? Why would you want to do that?" asked Chan.

"Let's say I was poaching eggs and then realized I didn't want them."

"Uh, geez," said Chan, "I don't know." I could see Chan struggling to think of a solution to my stupid question.

"Dude, I'm just kidding."

"Oh, okay," said Chan, "I wasn't sure if you were serious or messing around."

"Well, I was messing around with the whole 'how to un-poach an egg' thing, but I was serious on how to unscramble an egg."

The grocery store proposal was just one of the many bizarre things Chan did within the first month of living with him. Why would he even propose such a preposterous idea? I don't think he was trying to pull one over on us. I think he truly believed it to be a fair deal. Chan's actions would only get worse; it was the first month, after all, and this was just the beginning.

Chapter 7 - First Week of School: Awkward BBQ

At the end of the first week of school, we decided that we were going to have a roommate BBQ. The reason for the BBQ was to bond and to celebrate surviving the first week of school. I know it's not the biggest accomplishment, but college kids will find any excuse to celebrate. Chan and I were outside manning the grill while Alex and Drew gathered plates and utensils. Chan and I made some small talk. Small talk isn't really my thing, but I lived with the guy, so I had to make the effort and make the nice. I asked Chan how his first week of school had gone.

"Is it all what you expected?"

Chan turned over a steak and said, "It's really easy so far. I thought it would be harder. You know what I mean?"

"Well, it is only the first week. It'll probably be harder by the time midterms come around," I stated.

"Oh yeah, I'm not too worried about that. I should be okay as long as I study. You know what I mean?" said Chan.

Now, the phrase "You know what I mean?" is something that Chan would say after every time he voiced his opinion or criticized someone or something. I remember being so flabbergasted at something he said once, and then being annoyed that he tried to mask it with, "You know what I mean?" I said to him, "No, I don't know what you mean. What do you mean?" To which he responded with a blank stare. Anyway, I'm getting all worked up. Let's get back to the BBQ.

As we made small talk, Chan started chatting with me about girls and relationships. I had no desire to have this conversation. I tried to send him a hint by nodding my head and browsing Instagram, but he seemed oblivious to my body language and my obvious lack of interest. He continued to have a conversation with himself. He went on to tell me over and over how badly he wants a girlfriend. He would say things like, "At this stage in my life, I'm ready for one." He then went on to tell me about what a catch he is. I felt like I was on *The Bachelor* and Chan was pitching himself to me. Where is Chris Harrison to pull me away from this dude? Chan is not getting a rose.

I stopped giving Chan auditory responses; I just stuck with nodding my head.

"I can cook a girl anything! Who wouldn't want that? I'm going to be such a good husband," he babbled.

Meanwhile, I was losing my mind listening to him convince himself that he is husband material. As I was aimlessly nodding my head to Chan pretty much reciting his Tinder bio to me, I noticed an eyelash of mine had fallen out onto my arm. I pinched the escaped eyelash between my thumb and index finger. I brought it up to my eye level and made a wish. I then blew the lush lash into the wind, and hopefully away from the steaks. I made a wish for Alex and Drew to return and rescue me. It's normal to make a wish when your lashes fall out, right? That's, like, an established superstitious social norm? I'm not a weirdo for doing that. Guys, it's a thing. Chan proceeded to carry on this conversation with himself.

"Yeah, in high school, I never wanted a girlfriend, but now that I'm in college, I'm ready for it...you know what I mean?"

At this point, I was fully checked out and absorbed in my phone. By the time Alex and Drew finally arrived with the plates, even I felt desperate. Second-hand desperation kills. It's best not to flaunt it.

Chapter 8 - Pissed Off

The next Chanism isn't for the faint of heart. It is something that I hate having to share with you. But I, unfortunately, must. It's the only way you can truly understand the horrors of living with Chan. If you get grossed out by bodily functions, corn, or bits of carrots, then skip to the next chapter. If you do read this section and get grossed out, don't blame me. Blame Chan. After all, he's the one forcing me to do this. What a jerk!

This is the story of how I first discovered the next Chanism. Most days, I would ride home from class and carry my bike up our apartment steps. I would then proceed to carry the bike up the stairs in our apartment building. Once I was in our apartment, I would have to pop a wheelie and wheelie-walk the bike through our narrow hallway and then up our stairs, through Chan's loft/room, and into my room, where I would place my bike on the deck that was connected to my master bedroom. Quite the quest, just to put a bike away. Not to mention, the part about the rope bridge suspended over lava, and the dragons. This was a difficult task, and Chan refused to keep his bike anywhere but in the narrow hallway, hence why I had to wheelie-walk my bike, but I digress. The bike in the hallway wasn't a big deal. In fact, the bike in the hallway was the least of my worries.

After storing my bike on my balcony, I would use the en suite bathroom. This is my usual routine. I have a thing about public restrooms, so I hold it until I get home. I only go to the bathroom in public restrooms if my bladder levees are about to burst. I make an effort to avoid public bathrooms unless I'm at a Starbucks or a nice restaurant. The bathrooms at school were pretty bad. I once walked into a stall and found three gum wrappers, blood, a small bag of what I presumed was cocaine, and a banana. I would love to know how these items all came together. There's gotta be a story there. I think we, as people, have to make public restrooms great again. #MPRGA

When did it become socially acceptable to not flush? I shouldn't have to walk into a stall with someone's waste staring up at me. If you're going to pee in a stall, please lift the seat up and try to aim for the bowl. If you take one thing away from this book, please let this be it. I can't tell you how many times I walk into a restroom stall, only to be met with a pee-covered toilet seat and wonder, *What kind of person does that?!* People, be aware, these seat pee-ers are amongst us. They dress like us, act like us, and even look like us. But they are not us.

But, really, who does that? Enter, Chan.

Having locked up my bike, I rushed to the en suite bathroom (that means it's attached; keep up). In the bathroom, I found pee driblets on the toilet seat. My eyes zeroed in on them immediately. I felt my eye twitch and my hair turn gray. I quickly grabbed some toilet paper to dab the infected toilet seat. I then coated it with some disinfectant spray. I wiped it again with toilet paper. After that, I scrubbed it with a wet wipe. For a third time, I wiped it again with some toilet paper. Once the seat was uncontaminated, I "took the kids to the pool," so to speak. This is the time where I check emails, Snapchat, and Instagram. But this time was different. I couldn't do that. All I could focus on was figuring out who had desecrated the sanctity of my toilet seat. So, I sat and pondered about who the culprit could be. I had a real *True Detective* moment.

I had a hunch that it was Chan. His loft-room was adjacent to my master suite. It would have been convenient for him to use the restroom in my room instead of tracking downstairs. However, being the diplomatic person that I am, I decided to launch a thorough investigation. I asked Alex, when he returned, if he had used that bathroom. "Nope," he said. I told him that I discovered some pee on the toilet seat. He rolled his eyes and smirked. Judging from his response, I could tell he, too, thought the violator was Chan.

Later on, Alex, Drew, and I attempted to shoot some hoops (we're not very good). While we were shooting around, I asked Drew if he had peed on the toilet seat in my room.

"No, why would I do that?"

Drew's answer said so much. In the context of the question, Drew did not purposely or accidentally pee on the seat. But on a higher level, his answer brought forth a logical question. Who would do that? A careless person? Perhaps a blind person? A blind, careless person? But, seriously, who does that? Apparently, Chan. However, why would Chan accidentally pee on the toilet seat and not clean it up? Because if he didn't notice, then I'll give him the benefit of the doubt; accidents happen, yadda, yadda. Now, to break down the whole incident. How does one pee on the seat? In my mind, this can happen one of two ways. Option A: He pees with the toilet seat down, which we all know can have some splash-back depending on the DWD (Dick to Water Distance). Or option B: He sits while he pees, and when he stands up, some driblets escape. Wouldn't he turn around to flush? So, wouldn't he see the driblets then? Maybe this was a one-time thing, a glitch in the matrix.

Welp, that theory was out the door. It wasn't a one-time thing. Coming home from school to find pee driblets became an unfortunate part of my daily routine. I was ill fated to find the occasional poop remnants. To Chan's credit, he undoubtedly ate his vegetables. Once, the toilet situation was so bad I had to speak up. I spent an hour rehearsing what I was going to say to Chan. I wanted to be respectful but firm. Once I had my lines memorized, I walked into Chan's loft. He was listening to music. I waved to get his attention.

He took his headphones off and said, "Hello?"

"Hey, so you kind of left a mess in the bathroom. Can you clean it up?" I asked.

"Sorry. Sorry," said Chan. He got up and strolled into my bathroom and flushed. What a nice guy, right? Wrong. He would always apologize for any wrongdoing, but he merely said it as a reaction to end any issue, instead of resolving an issue. There was no sincerity to his apologies. When he walked past me, he apologized to me again. "Sorry."

Hmm, sorry didn't leave shit in the toilet bowl, I remarked to myself.

The pee driblets continued to show up on the toilet seat. I'd hoped my confrontation with Chan would instill more caution in his bathroom etiquette. Clearly, I had been wrong. So, I decided to take action. By action, I mean write a passive-aggressive note. I grabbed a Sharpie and yellow construction paper (appropriate, I know). I wrote, "KEEP THE BATHROOM NEAT, DON'T PEE ON THE SEAT." I wrote it in all caps, so he would know I meant business. I left the note on top of the tank that holds the water. I'm very passive and do everything in my power to avoid conflict. The reason I left the sign was that I was going to go home for the weekend, so if Chan did see the sign, I wouldn't have to deal with him inquiring about it.

When I returned from visiting my mom, I removed the sign. I don't know if Chan ever saw the note, but he never used my bathroom again. Which was unfortunate for Alex and any house guests. It's unfortunate because this meant Chan was using the downstairs bathroom that Alex and guests used. Chan continued to leave pee driblets on the toilet and poop remnants in the bowl. But that was Alex's problem now.

Chapter 9 - The Curry Incident of 2016

    This next story is one of my least fond memories of Chan, mainly because it ended up deflating my wallet. This event validated my suspicions that Chan is oblivious to common sense. This was the first big Chan incident of the year; the curry incident took place toward the end of my first month of living with Chan. People, please trim your fingernails before you read this next passage—Chan's behavior is a head scratcher. Safety first...Then teamwork.

    Alex and I were at the grocery store getting beer, wine, cheese, and some meat—you know, the essentials on the millennial food pyramid—while Drew and Chan were holding down the fort. This was Drew's last night with us, because he had found a room in a house that he was going to rent out. I figured this might bum Chan out, since he and Drew had bonded over their love of pot. I remember, one night, Drew telling me of a bond people form when they smoke pot together. Chan and Drew would smoke in the parking lot located out the back door of our apartment. (The apartment building is designed so everyone's back door faces the parking lot.) When we first moved in, Chan asked if he could smoke in the apartment, but Alex and I were very adamant that smoking in the apartment was not only not okay, but also a violation of our lease. Even so, during the duration of the first month, Drew and Chan had managed to form a magical marijuana bond. This is something I'll never understand, considering that I have never smoked anything in my life (I'll stick to drinking).

Alex and I returned home to find Drew sitting at our dining room table, grinding up some pot. He had a peculiar look on his face.

"So, do you guys wanna know what happened?"

Uh-oh, I thought. *What now?* Before I could verbally respond, I saw a giant, round, highlighter-yellow stain on the carpet. The stain was about the size of a personal pizza.

"Wait. What? How? How did this happen?" I exclaimed.

Drew perked up and said, "Chan made a giant bowl of yellow chicken curry." Keep in mind, Chan's portions are huge. "As he went to set his bowl on the coffee table, he placed the bowl half on the table, with the other half hanging over the edge. Annnnnnnnd, as you might expect, the giant bowl of curry flipped over onto the carpet."

I shook my head. Since the curry stain was still there, I asked the most logical question.

"Where is Chan?"

"Chan took off to the gym," said Drew, trying not to laugh.

I winced, then said, "So he spilled curry on the carpet and went to the gym instead of cleaning it up?"

"Yup, pretty much," said Drew.

Alex and I immediately opened up a bottle of wine. Had to calm the nerves with some Jesus Juice. Moments later, Chan walked in. His face was rosy, and he had sweat stains down his back.

"Hey," said Chan.

I looked at Chan and unenthusiastically responded with, "Sup?"

"So, what are you guys up to?" asked Chan.

Like a disappointed father, I crossed my arms and, in a condescending tone, said, "Just wondering what that is," whilst glancing at the pee-colored stain on the floor.

"Oh, yeah. I spilled some curry, but I didn't know what to do."

Alex, Drew, and I simultaneously made a face.

"Well, if I spilled curry, I would clean it right away, before the stain set," I said.

"Oh…how?" asked Chan, with unfortunate honesty.

I chuckled. "With carpet cleaner?"

"Do we have that?" he asked.

"No," I answered.

Alex and I have never had this problem, so it is no surprise we didn't have a spare bottle of carpet cleaner.

"Where would I get that?" he literally asked.

Seriously?!?!

"If I were you, I would go to the store, get carpet cleaner, and clean the stain," said Drew.

"What store?" he asked.

This guy is not doing himself any favors, I thought.

We all responded at once, "Target!"

Target was the closest store to our apartment that would 100 percent have carpet cleaner.

Chan put on a tiny shirt and fled to Target. Alex, Drew, and I sat in disbelief. After every one of these displays of obliviousness, I would find myself thinking time and time again, *Who does that?* and the answer was always the same. Chan. You see, Chan transcends common sense, because he doesn't have any sense, and for sense to be common, there needs to be an abundance of an established precedence of sense.

Chan returned back after twenty minutes at Target. He sprayed the already set stain and did his best to scrub the carpet. The carpet cleaner didn't help. So, Chan, like a responsible adult, said, "I'll pay whatever for the carpet to be replaced." (Remember this quote.)

Chan went to take a shower. Alex and I took turns trying to get the stain out. However, our efforts were not rewarded. We got creative and moved our area rug to cover the stain. Curry Stain 1, Us 0.

Chapter 10 - Soup for the Homeless

It was on a Friday at 5 a.m. when I was awakened by a rhythmic noise. I was tired and groggy. It took me a couple of seconds to figure out the source of the noise. It was jazz music, coming from Chan's room. Not that anything is wrong with jazz, but come on, dude. There is a time and a place. Luckily, the smooth jazz tunes were faint enough that I could sleep through them. Around two hours later, I awoke to the same music. I was annoyed for being up early on my class-free, sleep-in day.

I got up to make some coffee. I carefully opened the door that separates Chan's loft and my room. I was like a ninja. I was always considerate of waking people up in the apartment, which is why I was particularly annoyed that Chan wouldn't extend me the same courtesy. As I walked past Chan's large, half-naked body, I noticed his laptop next to him, blasting jazz music, for all the world to hear. Congratulations, Chan, you have single-handedly ruined jazz for me. Dick!

I continued with my morning routine, which consisted of multiple cups of coffee, oatmeal, checking emails, and social media. Later that morning, I went back downstairs to get my fourth cup of coffee. As I carefully opened my door in an effort to not wake the beast, I realized that the jazz music had stopped. Thank God! I assumed his battery had died. I was wrong. Chan had gotten up and turned it off. When I got downstairs, I was greeted by what Alex and I refer to as "The Butt Crack of Dawn." The Butt Crack of Dawn is Chan's butt crack, which is most known for making appearances in the morning while Chan eats his breakfast.

Chan ate his breakfast at a small wooden table, which tied in perfectly with our nautical decor. The table was pushed up against the back of the couch. If the seats on the couch were taken, this allowed us to eat and face the TV. Since we had a smaller table, we also had small chairs. These chairs were even smaller for Chan. Why he didn't just sit on the couch and use the coffee table is a mystery. These small chairs displayed Chan's butt crack beautifully, if you're into that sort of thing. It was an unfortunate thing to see every day. Chan's butt crack was clearly a morning person, and on this particular morning, I swear to God, I think it winked at me.

I hustled into the kitchen to escape the gaze of Chan's butt crack. While I was in there, Chan asked if I wanted to feed the homeless some soup. What an asshole. How dare he ask me a question that provokes numerous follow-up questions? Like, "Do you volunteer at a soup kitchen or shelter? Is the soup homemade or store bought? Do you think they're going to want soup when it's ninety degrees out? How long is this going to take?" Luckily, I had a project to work on. I told Chan that I couldn't help him because I was busy doing homework, working on a project all weekend.

He gave me a look of disappointment and then spoke in a soft, monotone voice: "Another time, then."

He turned around and went back to the table. As he turned, his butt crack gave me the same disappointed look. After throwing up a little bit in my mouth, I went upstairs to study and work on a group project that I would end up doing the majority of the work on. While trying to study, I could hear a bunch of pots and pans banging around the kitchen, with the occasional sound of a blender going off. It was like he was auditioning for Stomp. This racket went on for about an hour, with a five-minute blender solo at the end. Geez, and I thought this guy blasting jazz was irritating.

Chan had an annoying talent for finding ways to distract me, whether it be from sleep, studying, or TV. I put headphones on to silence Chan's cooking noises. I eventually went downstairs to get a coffee refill and check on Chan. God forbid he somehow locked himself in the oven (not that he would fit). When I got downstairs, Chan was shoving napkins and a pot of soup into an Ikea bag. You know, the big blue ones. He kindly asked if I would like to try his homemade soup. I said sure. He quickly poured me a bowl and fetched me a spoon. "Smells good," I said. He handed me the soup and stared as I sampled a spoonful. It was good, so I let him know just that.

"Soup's good."

Just at that moment, Alex and Drew walked through the door. Chan quickly recruited them to help him pass around soup to the homeless. To my surprise, they both agreed to go.

Chan then turned to me and asked if I wanted to go. I, again, told him that I couldn't go.

"Aw, c'mon," he said, pleading, "it'll probably only be an hour."

"I'm good," I said.

"Are you scared or something?" Chan said jokingly.

"Actually, I am. I'm scared of homeless people."

Chan gave me a confused face. "Why?"

"That came out wrong. I'm afraid of the germs that homeless people have," I explained.

"What do you think is going to happen?" he asked.

"I don't know...I could be spat on? I don't want to be put in that position. I'm more than willing to donate money to help the homeless. I just don't want the germs or parasites," I said.

He replied, "Oh, okay."

He finished packing up his stuff, then he, Drew, and Alex went off. I could tell he didn't understand. I, indeed, do have a little bit of a germ thing. I wouldn't say I'm a germaphobe, I'm just germ-conscious. I also have a very real fear of a homeless person sticking their finger(s) in my mouth. That fear is ranked right above being in the open ocean, and being trapped in a conversation with Gary Busey. However, this fear of germs immediately disappears if an attractive girl asks to share a drink or food. So, I'm selectively germ-conscious.

I walked into the kitchen, where I was presented with Chan's soup mess. The amount of soup that was sprawled

Spilled Curry

throughout our kitchen was ridiculous. I found soup on the counter, the stove, the floor, the fridge handle. There was so much soup left in the kitchen that I thought, *Is there any left to give away?* I was annoyed by the mess. In fact, I was going to clean the mess, but then I thought, *Why ruin the fun for Chan?* I carefully navigated my way out of the kitchen, dodging soup puddles like they were land mines. I would hate to get soup on my foot and track that on to the already stained carpet.

Now that the apartment was empty, I was able to drink coffee and read in peace. One of the assignments I had to get done by Monday was to read some poems from Walt Whitman's *Leaves of Grass*, and then select one to memorize and recite to the class on Monday. My high anxiety made this a very difficult. In an effort to make the upcoming excruciating experience as painless as possible, I planned to spend hours on this assignment. When I got halfway through the assignment, I heard the front door slam open. Is that possible? Anyway, the door being aggressively opened meant that Chan had returned, along with Alex and Drew.

Since Chan was back, I knew that there would be no chance for me to study peacefully in my room. I went down to see how the soup event had gone. To my surprise, Chan was nowhere to be found. Alex was putting on an episode of *Property Brothers* while Drew was grinding up some pot. I greeted them and then mouthed the words, "Where's Chan?"

"He just dropped off the Ikea bag and went home for the weekend," said Alex.

The vein in my forehead made its presence known. I became annoyed. "So, is he expecting us to clean up this soup mess?!"

"Fucking Chan, dude," said Drew, shaking his head.

I went on to frantically point out every soup spill in the kitchen. It's one thing to spill soup. I get it, accidents happen, gravity is at play. But to not even clean it up? Come on, dude.

"Remember how he didn't clean up the curry stain?" mentioned Alex. We were all dumbfounded.

After a few moments of silence, I said, "Speaking of soup, how was giving it to homeless people?" Drew and Alex looked at each other and laughed.

"Did you guys go to an underpass or St. James Park?"

"Yeah, we went to St. James Park," said Alex.

For those of you not familiar with San Jose, St. James Park is notorious for its homeless population.

"So, we get down there," said Alex, opening a Corona, "and Chan goes up to this scruffy-looking guy next to his bike and asks him if he would like some soup. The man asks Chan why, and Chan says, 'Oh, I'm giving soup out to the homeless.' And the guy says, 'I'm not homeless!'"

Despite being profiled as homeless, Alex told me that the guy helped direct them to actual homeless people.

"Did they want the soup? It's like ninety-five degrees out."

"Some people took it, others weren't interested," Alex told me.

"Tell 'm about the lady," said Drew, rolling up his joint.

"Oh, some lady started cursing out Chan when he tried to give her soup. She was a little crazy, though," said Alex as he twirled his index finger around his ear.

The guys and I spent the rest of the afternoon cleaning Chan's soup mess, along with the whole living room and dining room. We scrubbed the counters, stove, fridge, and the cabinets (yes, the soup was on the cabinets). We washed all the dishes, except for the dishes Chan used to make the soup. I mean, it was the least he could do.

I hadn't planned on cleaning Chan's mess, but since he was going to be away for the rest of the weekend, I didn't have much of a choice. Alex tackled the task of cleaning the bathroom that he and Chan shared, without a hazmat suit. Drew helped pick up the living room while I vacuumed. It was during this cleaning sesh that I noticed how much of Chan's stuff was scattered throughout the living room. In the living room, he had multiple socks, a shirt, pants, a backpack, and multiple shoes. We respectfully put all of his items in a pile and figured he'd get the message. We enjoyed what was left of our Chan-free Friday evening. Alex cooked some steaks while Drew and I sat on the couch and talked about life.

Following dinner, we spent the rest of the night drinking beer and watching home improvement shows on HGTV. After a couple of drinks, we got emphatic about the improvements we would make. After seeing the home featured on the show, our conversation would go something like this (keep in mind, we know nothing about home renovations, we just think we do):

Nick: "That wall next to the kitchen has got to go. I'm all about that open concept."

Drew: "Not if it's a load-bearing wall; then you gotta get a beam, and those are pricey."

Alex: "They could get laminate flooring instead of real hardwood to save money for the beam."

Nick: "Can we talk wallpaper?"

Alex: "What about it? It's shitty."

Nick: "It's obviously going to go on demo day, but would you do an accent wall in nice wallpaper or just do paint?"

Alex: "Paint."

Drew: "You guys hungry? I wanna make cookies."

Nick: "I'm down!"

Alex: "Me too!"

On Saturday afternoon, we went swimming and played basketball. Chan was gone and life was great. That evening, we hung out and watched a *Cops* marathon. After watching hours upon hours of *Cops*, I noticed a strange pattern. I noticed that 70 percent of the people arrested were wearing jean shorts. Keep an eye out the next time you see an episode of *Cops*; you'll notice this phenomenon too. The lesson here is, don't trust anyone in jean shorts. No one! I assume all people in jean shorts are guilty. At the very least, guilty of committing a crime against fashion.

Spilled Curry

Sunday morning, I was awoken by Chan aggressively opening the front door. Why can't he just turn the knob and walk through? Why does he have to fling it open until it bounces off the doorstop? This ruckus continued. I heard him fidgeting around in the kitchen. At first, I was annoyed to be woken up by Chan yet again. Then, the optimist in me thought that I could take advantage of this time that I would have been sleeping by reading the rest of *Leaves of Grass* and practicing my poem I had to memorize and recite in front of the whole class.

When noon came around, I took a break from studying and went downstairs to check in with everyone. Alex and Drew were watching *House Hunters*, while Chan was in his boxers, floating around the kitchen. Chan had an uncomfortable look on his face. He looked up from the sink and said, "Hey, guys, can you help me with the dishes?"

Alex quickly caved in and said sure. *Are you fucking serious? We spent hours cleaning up the soup mess you left! Along with the whole apartment. You have the audacity to ask for help with the dishes*? is what I wanted to say. I had one of those moments you see on TV, where a person is asked something by a person they don't like, and they imagine a scenario where they tell that person off or do something violent to them. Once I checked back into reality, I reluctantly said, "Sure. Even though I already cleaned earlier, I will help out with the dishes."

That evening, Alex and I drank beers and soaked in the hot tub. This hot tub would become a sanctuary where would retreat to decompress and vent about Chan. I was still mad about being asked to help with the dishes after being on my hands and knees scrubbing the floors. Alex didn't seem nearly as frustrated as I was. While I went on a rant about Chan, Alex nodded his head while he snapchatted a German girl. At the end of my gratuitously long rant, Alex looked up from his phone and said, "Don't worry about it. He's just a dumbass."

"That's the thing, I don't think he is stupid...He is…He's...He is just unaware...of almost *everything*."

I had an epiphany. Chan was oblivious. He was oblivious to organization and clutter created by him or others. Trying to logically label him is impossible. He operates on an illogical level. He does not abide by our normal social conventions. He's unknowingly gone rogue. I know what you're thinking: *Talk to him, voice your concerns*. We tried that. We had talks about minor issues. Chan is a delicate flower. So, when Alex and I would raise a concern, Chan would immediately say, "Oh sorry." Then, a few days later, he would forget the conversation and do the thing we asked him not to do. As you can see, that strategy is useless when it comes to Chan.

Just then, we heard the gate open. Alex and I both looked over to the gate, but it was too dark to see who was entering the pool area. All I could make out was a large silhouette. *Oh no*, I thought. *Did Chan follow us to the pool? Would he dare invade our Chan-free oasis? I can't believe the nerve of this guy.* As the figure approached, the dim light from the pool revealed that it wasn't Chan. It was a tubby, white

Spilled Curry

older man. He was wearing flip-flops, board shorts, and a gold chain that sat on his belly. He had a towel in one hand and a drink in the other.

"How you boys doin'?" he asked.

"We're good," I said.

"Mind if I join you fellas?" he asked. The man put his towel by the side of the pool and then put his phone on top of the towel. The old, tubby man took a sip of his drink and then said, "My name is Doug, by the way."

"Hey, Doug, I'm Nick. Nice to meet you."

"Hi, I'm Alex. Good to meet you," said Alex, looking up from his phone.

"Nice to meet you guys. How's the water?" asked Doug, who was sliding off his flip-flops.

"The water is warm," said Alex. Doug slid into the hot tub while balancing his drink in his hand.

"How's it going?" asked Alex.

"Not good," said Doug. "Not good at all. I'm sad today. I found out that one of my good friends was killed today."

Well, Doug instantly ruined the relaxing vibe of the hot tub. "Oh, I'm sorry for your loss," I said, trying to remember protocol when hit with sad news.

"Yeah, my friend was shot. So, I gotta make plans to fly out to New York to the funeral. He was a good guy." Doug sighed.

"Wow, I'm so sorry," I said.

"It's sad but that's life, though. You guys go to State?" Doug asked.

"Yeah," I said.

"You guys like it?" he asked.

"Yeah, for the most part," I said.

"School's good and the area is nice," added Alex.

"It didn't always used to be nice," murmured Doug. "Back in the day, there were knuckleheads on every block. I had to hire some guys to knock some heads in. You know, to clean up the neighborhood."

Oh my God! Is this guy a mobster? I mean, he was wearing a chain in a hot tub, which is one of the most gangster things I have ever seen.

Doug's mood seemed to change drastically. After boasting about hiring thugs to beat up other thugs, he got quiet. After some uncomfortable silence soaking in the tub like a dirty dish in a sink, Doug, with no context, said, "I should have been a better father."

I looked at Alex and he looked back me. We both knew we were in for an ear full. *How do you respond to that statement?*

I just said, "Oh."

"I just got caught up in my business and life," Doug said. This unprovoked statement was followed by an immediate and chilling silence. By chilling, I mean Doug not only brought the mood down, the hot tub temperature fell a few degrees as well. "You guys would love my daughter. Don't worry, she takes after her mother. A real beauty. I would show you a picture, but I don't want to see you guys eyeballing her."

He then put his drink by the lip of the pool and picked up his phone. "I'll show you a picture of my lady."

I was amused watching Doug struggle to swipe through photos with his soaking-wet hand. *Dude, why bring a towel if you're not going to use it?* Finally, Doug caught on and ran his wet finger through his towel.

"What do you guys think about her?" he asked, shoving his damp phone in our faces. On his phone was a picture of a middle-aged Asian woman.

"She looks good," I said, trying to please Doug.

"Yeah, I think I'm going to marry her. You guys like music?"

This guy likes to jump from topic to topic like a news anchor.

Yeah, who doesn't like music? I thought. *Has anyone answered that question with 'no'? That question is almost redundant. Really, if someone truthfully responded to that question with a no, then are they even worth talking to?* Alex and I both responded to Doug with, "Yes."

"You guys like Neil Young?"

Alex and I were quiet, both trying to figure out who Neil Young was.

"I know the name," I said.

"You guys really don't know him? He's a legend. He is one of my good friends too," Doug said. "I have a couple of his guitars. You guys should come over sometime and check out some of my instruments."

"Oh cool," I said, nodding my head. I knew full well there was no way I would let myself be anywhere near Doug again, let alone in his apartment. His moods swings and mobster persona were too much. He told us he hired dudes to hurt other people! There was just no way.

Doug then, without a request, began to play us Neil Young music for the next ten minutes. He turned his phone sideways and rested the side of it on his belly. This meant half of his phone was submerged in the hot tub without a case. As we listened to some Neil Young with DJ Doug, two young Indian men approached the hot tub.

"Hi, Mr. Doug!" one of them said.

"Hi-yah," responded Doug.

Doug began conversing with them for a while. During this time, Alex and I zoned out for a bit to take a break from Doug, Chan, and life.

I overheard one of the Indian men say, "It must be great to be you, Mr. Doug. You are rich and have a very cool car."

Doug seemed uncomfortable talking about his money and car, but ask him about being friends with Neil Young, and he was an open book. After their conversation, the hot tub was a quiet sausage fest. The Indian men began talking back and forth in Hindi to each other. As they conversed, Doug stared at them. After a couple minutes, Doug retorted, "I KNOW WHAT YOU'RE SAYING!"

All eyes focused on Doug. This hot tub of horror got even more awkward. It grew uncomfortably quiet. The silence was broken when one of the men spoke up and said, "Mr. Doug, we didn't say anything bad."

Doug looked at them, and they nervously stared back. Doug finally responded, "I know. I just wanted to let you know that I understand what you're saying."

Geez, Doug, way to put me on pins and needles. I thought they were trash talking you, and you could understand. All that awkwardness and tension for that? Then again, he did tell us his friend was shot within the first minute of meeting him.

"Yeah, I work with a lot of Indians in my line of work, so I have learned the language," he explained. Just then, the Neil Young tunes stopped playing. Doug's phone had drowned. He picked his phone off his belly and shook it.

"Damn phone," he said, dabbing it with a towel. "Well, I gotta go." He got out of the pool, said, "Take care, fellas," and grabbed his stuff. As he exited the pool area, I couldn't help but feel bad for him. He lost a friend and an iPhone in the same day.

After hanging out in the hot tub, I went to my room to study. I did have a poem to memorize, after all. I stood in front of my mirror, rehearsing Walt Whitman's "The Ship Starting." This task increased in difficulty when my concentration was broken by Chan's hyena-like laughter. It was loud and high pitched. While I struggle to memorize this poem, Chan wailed at funny YouTube videos. Again, I was forced to put headphones on to block the unwanted Chan noises.

I arose early and completed my morning routine and then departed for school. I arrived early to rehearse my poem. In class, the professor assigned us an order in which we would perform. I was hoping to be last, but that was not the case. I was number fourteen out of a class of thirty-five. The professor was judging the presentations on these criteria: posture, delivery, and memorization. After about forty minutes, it was my turn.

I slowly walked up to the front of the class. As I looked out across the classroom, I was met with an absurd amount of eye contact. All eyes were on me. My mind went blank. I took a deep breath, and then exhaled. A wave of confidence consumed me. It was similar to the transformation Bugs Bunny makes in *Space Jam*. During the game against the Monstars, when he drinks MJ's "Secret Stuff." After my deep breath, I stood with statuesque posture and introduced myself.

"Hi, my name is Nick Rafter, and the poem I chose to recite for you is 'The Ship Starting.'"

I then stumbled through the first line. It got better from there. I got into a rhythm and picked it up, and had a strong finish.

Once class was over, I thought, *That wasn't so bad. I did a pretty good job.* Just then, I looked down and saw that my zipper was down. I mean, all the way down. The jeans I was wearing created a glory hole for all of my classmates to see. I was embarrassed, but then I thought, *Ya know, it could be worse.* At least I was wearing boxers.

Chapter 11 - "I Think I'm Dying"

Now that our apartment was clean, Alex wanted to use this opportunity to invite some friends over. While Alex was on the phone, coordinating with our friends, Chan busted through the door. Chan walked in with a box of junk and a bong. As he huffed and puffed, he managed to set his stuff down and say in an exhausted voice, "Look what my sister got me for my birthday." He grabbed his bong and presented it like a fisherman does a trophy fish. Alex sauntered into his room and closed the door. I couldn't care less about the bong, but I put on a smile and acted interested.

"Wow, that's so cool," I said in an unimpressed tone.

"Is Drew here?" asked Chan.

"No, he won't be here until the evening," I answered.

"I'ma try it with him," said Chan, pointing to the bong. He then clutched the bong like an academy award winner does an Oscar and trotted upstairs to watch Fox News.

Alex came out of the room to let me know that our friend from high school, Max, and his brother, Jake (who is also our friend), would be coming over. I was excited to see Max because he was in town visiting from UCLA. This would be my only time to see him before the next break. Even though the apartment was fairly clean, Alex and I wanted to do a quick scrub before Jake and Max arrived. We vacuumed, and wiped down the counters and coffee table. We also lit some candles to create an inviting ambiance. Just then, the front door opened, and Drew walked in. "What are the candles for?" asked Drew, pulling earbuds out of his ears.

Alex responded with excitement, "Max and Jake are coming over!"

"Oh, dope," said Drew.

Before Drew could put his backpack down, Chan appeared in his face and presented his bong.

"LOOK what my sister gave me for my birthday."

Drew's eyes lit up. He had the look of a kid on Christmas morning.

"Let's hit that shit," cheered Drew.

Chan, looking at Alex and me, asked, "Can we smoke it in here or should we go out back?"

Alex and I simultaneously directed, "Out back!"

Chan and Drew scurried out back. A few moments later, our apartment was filled with marijuana…smoke? Vapor? I don't know how bongs work. Chan and Drew had left the back door open, allowing a light breeze to blow the weed odor into the apartment.

Alex hustled to the back door and yelled, "If you're going to smoke back here, keep the damn door closed!"

Chan turned to Drew and commented, "I can never tell if he is joking." (He wasn't.)

Alex and I don't have a problem with marijuana, we just didn't want it smoked in the house. Our unit was in the center of the complex, which meant there was a lot of foot traffic in our area. If someone filed a complaint, it could jeopardize our lease. Trying to find a new apartment halfway through the semester was not on our bucket list. Also, if it is something you want to do, don't let it affect other people. We shouldn't have to be dodging clouds of smoke and odor to enjoy our overly expensive apartment.

Drew and Chan returned to the apartment, both coughing. Chan went up to his room to stream the latest Trump speech, while Drew watched an episode of *Cops* with me and Alex. During the *Cops* theme song, there was a knock at the door. Alex jumped up and let Max and Jake in. We flocked to the couch and watched sports. Alex yelled up at Chan, "Hey, Chan, come say hi."

Chan peeked over the loft edge down at us. "Hey," said Chan.

"Yo!" said Max.

"Sup," said Jake.

Chan walked downstairs into the living room, wearing only an uncomfortably small pair of boxers. I could tell our guests were taken aback by Chan's casual attire. Anybody would be unpleasantly surprised by meeting someone in underwear for the first time. Chan broke the awkward silence by asking if they wanted to use his new bong with him.

"Oh, yessir," said Max.

Jake, Max, Chan, and of course, Drew went out back to use the bong. Alex soon followed them out back to chat.

I stayed inside and sat on the couch by myself. I had some anxiety about them getting caught and didn't want to be a part of it. After about fifteen minutes, the guys came back, smiling and laughing. This sight brought with it a feeling of exclusion. I relate the feeling to walking up to a group of laughing people, and you so badly want to laugh just to feel included. Unfortunately, you can't laugh, because you did not hear the joke.

We ordered take-out and watched whatever sport was being played on ESPN. After dinner, we heard some shuffling around coming from Chan's loft. This shuffling around would come in intervals. On, off; on, off. It was very distracting. Eventually, Alex yelled up at the loft, "Everything okay up there?"

There was no response. A few moments later, a confused-looking Chan wandered into the living room, grasping his love handle. Chan, with a serious, yet confused face, said, "Guys, I think I'm dying."

Max, trying not to laugh, said, "What now?"

"My side hurts. I think I'm dying," Chan said.

Alex rolled his eyes.

"Seriously, guys, I think I'm having a heart attack," said Chan, pointing to his love handle.

"That's not where your heart is," I replied.

"I'm too young to die," responded a frightened Chan. Clearly, the bong had taken its toll on Chan. He had smoked so much weed that he had become paranoid.

Trying to contain my laughter, I said, "Look, that's where your kidney is, so if anything, you're having a kidney attack."

Chan looked even more frightened.

"Is that a thing?" asked a frantic Chan, rubbing his kidney as if it were a magic lamp.

"It's not a thing. You probably smoked too much weed. Why don't you have a glass of water and then go lay down for a bit and see if you feel better?" I offered.

"Oh, okay...my side hurts and I am too young to die," he said.

"Maybe you have kidney stones? Just lay down for a bit," I told him.

"Oh no! People in my family have kidney stones. Maybe it's in my genes?" said Chan.

"I don't know if it's hereditary or not. It's probably nothing; just try to relax and lay down," I assured him.

"Dude, you're fine!" said Alex, who was struggling to enjoy the game.

At this point, everyone was unamused with Chan's paranoia. Even Chan had had enough. He walked up to his loft. He did that thing kids do when they don't get their way, walking with his head down and his shoulders shrugged. Fortunately for our sanity, we didn't hear from Chan the rest of the night.

The next morning, Alex and I got up early to buy bagels and coffee for everyone. Jake and Max had spent the night, and we didn't have any breakfast food. Who's got the time for breakfast when you're constantly trying to make it to class on time? When we got back, Drew was grinding up some pot while Max and Jake played Xbox.

"Chan left," said Drew.

"Where did he go?" asked Alex.

"He went to the hospital to check out his kidneys," said Drew, packing the ground-up weed into the bong.

"No way!" I exclaimed.

"Yeah, I heard him on the phone with his parents, and then he was on the phone with the...the—what are they called?"

"Advice nurses?" I asked.

"Yeah," said Drew.

"It would suck to have kidney stones," said Alex.

"BRB," said Drew, as he got up to go smoke out back.

"Yeah, I hear it's very painful," I said.

Alex sat on the couch next to Max and Jake, who were in a heated online match of 2K basketball.

"Don't you have to physically pee the stone out?" muttered Alex through a mouthful of bagel with cream cheese.

"Hmm, I think so," I said.

"Geez, if I had a kidney stone, I would be pissed," noted Alex.

In this case, the only thing that was pissed was the kidney stone from Chan's urethra.

Chapter 12 - Chan, The Human E.M.P.

"Hello?" I said upon entering the apartment. "Helloooo, anybody home?" No reply. *Huh, I must be the first one back from Thanksgiving break.* I went to the fridge to store some leftover turkey and pies my mother had sent with me. Peeking out from underneath the fridge was a whole green onion stalk. *Goddammit, Chan, how do you not notice dropping a vegetable on the floor?* Naturally, I moved the green onion to the middle of the kitchen floor to see if Chan would notice it and throw it away. I also snapped a pic and sent it to Alex.

After putting my leftovers away, I decided to unload the dishwasher. I pulled out a bowl to find rice caked on the inside, so I scrubbed it and set it aside for the next load. The next bowl I grabbed had food in it as well. I then grabbed a plate, which also had food on it. *What is happening right now? Did Chan not prewash anything? Are you kidding me right now? Now I have to scrub all these dishes and run them again.* I accused Chan because he was the last one to leave the apartment before Thanksgiving break. Also, let's be honest. Who else would commit such a diabolical act like not pre-washing the dishes? Fucking Chan, man! After scrubbing all the dishes, I ran them again. Thank God for steel wool.

I began drafting a lengthy text to Alex with photos of the dishes that Chan had attempted to wash. Sometimes I would take photos of Chan's messes around the apartment and send them to Alex. I found it to be a therapeutic way to vent my frustration with Chan. When I was on paragraph three of my text draft, I began to catch whiffs of a burning smell. I got up off the couch and began sniffing around the apartment like a bloodhound. The smell led me to the kitchen. Eventually, I located the burning smell, emanating from the dishwasher. I got freaked out because I had recently learned it was possible for dishwashers to catch fire. Over winter break, my mom's dishwasher control panel burned out. We later discovered her dishwasher had been recalled a few years earlier.

With the fear of the dishwasher being defective, I turned it off and unplugged it. I sent Alex another lengthy text about the dishwasher being broken. I then sent a maintenance request to the property manager. In their response, I was instructed to unplug the dishwasher, and that they would send someone in the morning. The next morning, around 9 a.m., there was a knock at the door. I let Juan, the repair guy, in and asked how he was doing, but this guy was all business. He went right to the dishwasher. I explained the burning smell. He poked around the inside of the dishwasher for a few moments, then closed the washer door and started the machine. After about five minutes, the burning smell wafted out of the dishwasher again. Juan seemed surprised, even though I had explained the situation in the maintenance request.

"I'm going to have to talk to my supervisor, but it seems like we are probably going to get you a new dishwasher. I'll be back tomorrow with my supervisor," said Juan in a very concerned voice. "In the meantime, do not run the dishwasher."

The next morning, Juan was back to check out the dishwasher.

"My supervisor, Dave, will be over shortly. In the meantime, I'll check it out again," said Juan, pointing to our dishwasher. Juan got out a flashlight and then groaned as he got on all fours. "Ope, fixed it," said Juan.

"What? Really?" I exclaimed.

"Yeah, look at this," said Juan, grabbing a chopstick off the bottom of the dishwasher. This chopstick had been on the coil that heats the dishwasher. "See," said Juan, pointing to a scorch mark on the chopstick. He handed me the chopstick and then took out his walkie. "This is Juan for Dave. The dishwasher issue for unit 2204 has been resolved." Juan put his walkie back into his holster.

"That was a quick fix," I said.

"Yeah, just be careful about the chopsticks falling through the rack in the dishwasher."

"Will do, and thanks for all your help," I said gratefully.

"Mhmm," said Juan, as he nodded his head. Juan then left to get to another job in the complex.

I sent Alex a text to inform him that we were not going to get a new dishwasher. I also sent him a picture of the

83

scorched chopstick. I felt bad for wasting Juan's time. I also was mortified Juan thought I was the culprit. I had been the only one home when Juan was over. Chan and Alex were both back home, visiting their families. He probably thought the chopstick was mine.

In this brief moment of reflection before I went to the gym, I thought about how fortunate we were after starting the dishwasher. After starting the dishwasher, I wouldn't have been there to smell the chopstick burning. A fire could have potentially started. All because Chan insisted on washing chopsticks in the dishwasher. After every load, a majority of the chopsticks would fall through the rack on to the bottom of the dishwasher. I think it would be easier to wash them by hand. Unfortunately, this wouldn't be the last fire-related incident involving Chan.

A little over a week after the chopstick incident, I was carrying a load of laundry to our machine. Our washer and dryer were located in the hallway adjacent to the bottom of our stairs. While approaching the machine, I nearly slipped on one of Chan's rogue socks. Chan was too lazy to keep his hamper in his room. To make his life easier, he would keep his hamper in the hallway next to the laundry machine. If that wasn't annoying enough, his socks and underwear somehow always managed to spill over into the hallway. We would have to tread carefully, like one does in the jungles of Nam. If too much laundry spilled over, we would just kick it into a pile.

After my close call with Chan's sock mine, I made it safely to our machine. I opened the lid to find it filled to the brim with whites, lights, coloreds, and towels. Chan was notorious for leaving his laundry in the machine. He would start a load and leave for hours, forcing me and Alex to move his laundry over to the dryer. After a while, Alex and I just piled his wet laundry on top of the dryer, forcing Chan to dry them himself. Chan always seemed to be doing laundry. His hamper never seemed to be empty. You would think, at some point, all his laundry would be clean except for the clothes he was wearing, but that was never the case. It was a constant loop of him doing laundry all the time. The strange thing was that he only wore cargo shorts and an unfortunately small t-shirt. His daily wardrobe was that of Bart Simpson. So why did he have so much laundry? This perplexed and vexed me. I placed my basket of laundry down to find Chan.

Chan was in the living room, eating and watching TV with Alex.

"Hey, Chan, when you get a chance, can you run your laundry so I can do mine after?"

"Oh, yeah, sorry," said Chan, with a mouth full of food.

Once Chan finished his food, he started his load of laundry and then went upstairs to play video games. Alex and I hung out and watched an episode of *House Hunters*. If you're not familiar with *House Hunters*, it's a show where people choose one of three houses from which they tour to live in. During house tour number two, Alex and I heard a clanking noise. It sounded like a car having some trouble starting.

Alex and got up and went to investigate. It didn't take us long to locate the sound; it was coming from the overly stuffed washing machine.

I looked up the stairs and said, "Hey, Chan, I think you broke the washing machine!"

"Huh?!" said Chan in a worried voice. He came downstairs, and right as he stood in front of the clanking washing machine, it shut off.

"Uh oh," said Alex.

"Yup, that's definitely broken," I said smugly.

"What should I do? I didn't mean to break it," squeaked a panicked Chan.

Well, obviously, you didn't break the machine on purpose, I thought. *There was no accusation of that*. I was enjoying seeing Chan act like a fish out of water, floundering around.

"You will have to file a maintenance report," said Alex.

"I don't even know how this happened," said Chan.

Really?! I thought. *The machine is filled to the fucking brim!*

"I mean, it's probably over-filled," I said in a calm but condescending tone.

"That can happen?" asked Chan, who was flustered. At this point, he had a pink hue to his face. "I never wanted this to happen," said Chan. "I didn't want to be the one to do this."

What the fuck is this guy's problem? I thought. The intent wasn't being called into question here. Common sense, however, was being called into question. One would think that it would be obvious to not overfill a washing machine, but common sense is an unfortunately foreign concept to Chan.

Chan emptied his damp clothes into his basket. He didn't seem to notice a pair of his wet boxer shorts had spilled over onto the floor. He then proceeded to go back upstairs to return to his video game. I decided to test my luck and take advantage of the empty washing machine. I put a reasonable amount of clothing into the machine. What do you know—the machine started up, no problem. The reason the machine hadn't worked for Chan was that there had been so much laundry in the machine that it had jammed the center part that stirred the clothes.

"Hey, Chan!" I yelled up the stairwell. "The washing machine is fixed. No need to send a report to maintenance!"

"It's fixed?" said Chan in a relieved voice.

"Yeah, it was just too many clothes for the machine to handle," I said.

"Oh, wow," responded Chan. "Thanks for fixing it. I was afraid I was going to have to buy a new one, ya know what I mean?"

"Oh yeah," I said, trying not to provoke any further conversation. I didn't want to get into the fact that all maintenance is covered by our outrageous amount of monthly rent.

It was the week before winter break. Alex and I were cleaning the apartment. Chan was in the kitchen, loading the dishwasher and watching some obnoxiously loud Japanese game show on his cell phone. I also picked up the green onion off the floor. Chan never noticed it. If he did, he didn't connect the dots and realize it was his.

"What are you guys doing?" asked Chan, who was staring at us from the kitchen.

"Just cleaning," I said, taking a break from scrubbing the hallway floor.

"Why?" asked a grinning Chan.

"Some of us like the house clean," barked Alex.

I looked up at Chan and calmly said, "It's just that we are going to be busy next week, studying for finals, so we are cleaning the house now. That way, after finals, we can pack up and go be on vacation."

"Oh," said Chan.

To my surprise, Chan got the urge (or the guilt) to pitch in. He grabbed some wipes and scrubbed some smudges on the wall that had been caused by him leaning his bike against it. Our hallway was pretty crowded. Between Chan's laundry pile and bike, navigating the hallway was challenging. It seemed Chan had turned over a new leaf. This gesture was a step in the right direction. He was actually participating in cleaning the apartment. I felt like a proud father. *My little Chan is finally learning.* Or so I thought. Chan went into the kitchen and, with one hand, grabbed a pot of leftover Kung Pao chicken from the night before. In the other hand, he held his phone so he could continue to watch his Japanese game show. Chan walked over to the trash can and stepped on the pedal that opens the lid. In one fluid motion, he tipped the pot over the trashcan to dispose of the leftover Kung Pao chicken. However, Chan was so enthralled with his show that he missed the trash can altogether and poured the Kung Pao chicken directly onto the carpet.

Chan was not fazed by his error. He casually retrieved the stain remover from underneath the sink. He sprayed the Kung Pao stain and then returned to watching his show and doing the dishes. This stain would join the infamous curry stain in the desecration of our carpet. This was due to the fact that Chan did not scrub the stain after spraying it. I'm not sure if he forgot how stain remover works, or just didn't care.

I mouthed to Alex, "Did he just dump the Kung Pao chicken on the floor?" in an effort to not let Chan hear. Alex nodded his head. While Chan was running the garbage disposal, Alex flipped him off. Just then, the garbage disposal made a strange noise.

"Uhh," murmured Chan.

"Is the garbage disposal working all right?" I asked.

"It's being weird," said Chan. He then began to rapidly flip the switch on and off.

"You break that too?" muttered Alex.

"Huh?" said Chan, trying to talk over the sound of our garbage disposal dying.

"He asked if the disposal was broken," I said. After a second, I added, "Can you turn it off? Having it run continuously isn't going to fix it."

"Oh, okay," said an unfazed Chan.

"Can one of you email maintenance?"

"Sure," said Alex reluctantly.

That night, things got hot in the hot tub. I don't mean hot like a one-on-one date on *The Bachelor*. I mean hot as in heated. Alex and I were just trying to relax and vent about Chan pretty much breaking every appliance we own.

"The guy's a walking E.M.P.," I said.

"What's an E.M.P.?" asked Alex, looking up from his phone.

"Never mind," I said. Then a thought struck me, and I said, "I bet you it's a cucumber."

"What?" asked Alex.

"Put your phone down for a sec. I think the garbage disposal is clogged with a cucumber. I pulled half a cucumber out last week," I explained.

"Ha. He always puts carrots and celery in there too," he added.

"So, what I'm getting from this conversation is that we both agree that Chan is at fault for breaking the disposal," I said.

"Pretty much," agreed Alex. Alex then went back to Snapchatting girls on his phone. Alex would Snapchat people by our pool area to let them (girls) know that he has access to a pool area.

The next day, Alex and I were hanging out after our finals. We were reenacting a scene from *Cops* when Chan strolled in.

"Hey," said Chan with a quizzical face. "What are you guys doing?"

"I'm the bad guy," I said.

"And I'm the cop," announced Alex.

"Okay?" said Chan, throwing his backpack against the wall. He then unbuttoned his pants and did a little shimmy to assist them in dropping to the floor. He then, in one motion, stepped out of his pants and pulled off his shirt. He followed that by doing this thing with his socks where he pulls the socks down past the heel but leaves the socks on his toes. Thus, utilizing half the sock. I don't know the purpose for this half-sock fashion statement. Maybe his toes are cold, and his heels are hot? This strange disrobing habit was part of Chan's daily routine when he would return from school.

He then went upstairs to watch Trump campaign videos. This was another strange component of his daily routine.

"Hahaha!" cackled Chan from his loft. Chan loved this classic bit Donald Trump would do. Donald would order security to remove protesters from a rally and say things like, "Get 'em outta here! Get 'em outta here!" This seemed to really get the crowd going, and Chan. I found the bit repetitive. It's like, talk about legitimate policies for once. A few moments later, our ears were invaded again with Chan's high-pitched laughter.

"Ahahaha!" howled Chan. "Ahahah!" He was laughing hysterically. Chan was pretty much crying from laughter. I couldn't understand how someone could find a very unfunny thing so funny. I didn't get it. This video that Chan found so hilarious was a clip of Donald Trump mocking a disabled reporter. I know this because Chan liked to sit in front of his computer and watch videos on full volume. This made watching our show nearly impossible.

Just then, there was a knock at the door.

"Maintenance," he yelled out. I answered the door. "Hey, I'm Dave, and I'm here to fix the disposal," he stated.

"Oh, okay," I said, gesturing my hand toward the kitchen. Alex, Dave, and I were making small talk when Dave suddenly glanced over and made a face. Naturally, I looked over to see what had affected Dave in this way. It was Chan, staring at Dave, in his boxers and his socks that only covered up half his feet. Dave was a trooper. After being caught off guard by Chan, he just rolled with the weirdness. Soon, all of us were watching Dave use this device that looked like a *Star Wars* droid on the disposal.

"Well, I'm almost done. Just be careful of the things you put in there."

"I will," said Chan. "Though, at my parent's house, I put whatever in their disposal. I even put paper towels." Everyone but Chan cringed. "What?" said Chan. "They have a really good disposal."

Essentially, he was using the garbage disposal as a trash can. I wasn't surprised by Chan's reveal. I had grown numb to Chan and his Chanisms. He managed to break every appliance he touched. The one solace of good news was that winter break was a week away and we desperately needed a break from school...and Chan.

Chapter 13 - The Coffee Shack Girl Returns

I parked my bike outside the business building with two hours to kill before my Alternative Film class final. I was to do a group presentation on British film director Andrea Arnold. With my first free hour, I was going to get coffee and a muffin while I listened to a podcast. With my second spare hour, I was going to meet with my presentation group to go over material and rehearse for our presentation. I felt great and I looked great. I was well dressed and well groomed. I even wore one of those trendy Lokai bracelets. Supposedly, the live Lokai bracelet contains mud from the Dead Sea and water from Everest. Very cool, which made me feel cool. I was in the zone and ready to present. I was hoping that the coffee shack girl would be working, whose name I had learned was Nicole. This would be a great opportunity for Nicole to see me at my best. In my eyes, this was a win-win scenario. I looked professional enough to give a presentation, and maybe also good enough to get Nicole, the "coffee shack girl," to notice me. What could go wrong?

I confidently approached the coffee shack and, to my delight, Nicole was working. I couldn't have scripted it better myself. Everything was going according to plan. Nicole came over to the counter.

"Hi," she said.

"Hey, can I have a coffee and a cookie, please?"

"Would you like room for cream?" she asked.

"Yes, please!" This seems to be going well. I was doing my best to be as cordial and polite as possible.

"Will that be all?" asked a beaming Nicole.

"Yeah, that'll do it."

"Your total is three dollars and fifty cents." I handed her my debit card. "Oh, I like your bracelet," she said as she handed my card back.

I froze for what felt like an eternity. I was scrambling for something to say.

Nicole had thrown me a curveball and I resented her for it. *She likes my bracelet? Who says that? What does that mean? Does that mean something? Or does she simply just like my bracelet?* My confidence rapidly dwindled. I had so many questions racing through my head. But I had to say something quickly before things got awkward. *Hurry, Nick! You desperately need to say something. You have almost crossed the awkward threshold! Say something, man!*

"There's cool stuff in there!" I blurted out, pointing to my bracelet. Before Nicole could respond, I put my head down, spun one hundred and eighty degrees, and walked away.

In hindsight, a simple "thank you" to Nicole complimenting my bracelet would have sufficed. Or, perhaps, just explaining what the "cool stuff" was. That was the last time I ever spoke to Nicole, the coffee shack goddess.

I usually drank my coffee within eyeshot of the coffee shack, but I had to get out of there. I ate my cookie and sipped my coffee outside my classroom. After I finished my cookie and coffee, Karen, a girl from my presentation group, arrived. We went over the material and waited for the rest of our group to get there.

"So, we are not presenting today," said Karen.

"We're not?" I said in a confused tone.

"Yeah. Check your email."

I quickly opened my inbox to find an email that read: *Dear students, on behalf of your instructor David Todson, I am writing to notify you that he must regretfully cancel today's 3 p.m. class as a result of a car accident that he was in on his way to the university. He has assured me that he will be in touch with you about your presentations and final exam, and sincerely apologizes for any inconvenience this unfortunate situation may cause you today. - Nancy*

"No way!" I exclaimed.

"That's so sad," said Karen.

"Yeah. Talk about a case of the Mondays," I said, jokingly. Karen didn't laugh.

I mentioned that because our previous Monday class had been cancelled due to another unfortunate incident. One minute before class began the previous week, we received an email that read: *Sorry for the late notice. En route to SJSU, got sick to stomach (leftover lunch?) and I am now in a Fremont auto dealership, sitting in their lobby, keeping close to the bathroom, if you know what I mean. Stay tuned for our last class. Sorry for not seeing you today! - David*

Poor guy was having a streak of bad luck.

"Hope he's alright," I said, breaking the silence.

"Me too," said Karen.

"Well, I guess we can go then," I said. "I'll be in touch about the project stuff."

"Okay, bye," said Karen.

Man, I thought to myself, *why couldn't he get in an accident like an hour earlier? Could have saved me from embarrassing myself in front of the lovely Nicole.*

I met with Alex back at the apartment. We packed and grabbed some last-minute items before we left home for winter break. Chan was watching footage of a pro-Trump rally. I yelled up at Chan from the living room, "Hey, Chan, we are going to leave for winter break. Please lock up when you leave; I would hate to return to find my Mac stolen."

"Okay, see you guys later. Enjoy the break!" yelled Chan.

"Enjoy your break, too, and congrats on your first semester of college," I said.

"Thanks," replied Chan.

"Oh, just remember to lock up when you leave," I said, fake smiling.

"Kay," responded Chan.

I was very serious about Chan locking up. The guy was a wild card. Who does not think about things like that? I am a high-anxiety individual who always worries about that, amongst other things.

Chapter 14 - The Beginning of the Second Semester

I was walking up the stairs to my apartment, wondering if Chan kept good on his word by locking up the apartment. The thought of him forgetting had bugged me all winter break. Standing in front of the door, I turned to Alex, whom I had caught a ride with, and said, "Moment of truth."

I turned the knob and it snagged. It was locked. Thank God. Alex and I walked into the apartment, only to be punched in the face by a foul smell. The smell was a potent stench that you could taste. It was like lying in bed with someone who farts and then pulls the cover over you. Thus, forcing you to endure the smell. Alex and I quickly pinched our noses to ease the suffering. We took a few seconds to recalibrate and assess the situation. Like first responders, we jumped into action. I quickly opened the back door and Alex opened all the windows.

We quickly, after some good detective work, ruled out Chan shitting on the carpet (due to the lack of evidence). We discovered the smell was coming from this small, aluminum compost bin Chan had purchased. He had forgotten to empty it before leaving. After losing in a round of rock-paper-scissors,

I had the task of opening the compost bin. As I reached for the lid, I thought, *Should I quickly open up the lid? Or, should I slowly open the lid?* I slowly removed the lid to find a small pile of eggshells. The container reeked. I told Alex to call an exorcist. I quickly held my breath and moved the compost bin out back. Alex and I grabbed some Febreze bottles and crop-dusted the entire apartment.

Chan bought this compost bin to put his food scraps in. This was somewhat redundant, on account of our apartment building not having a green compost bin. It was all going to the trash. So, Chan was just storing rotting food instead of throwing it out, even though it would just end up in the dumpster with the trash. This was a classic Chan move.

Later that evening, my and Alex's viewing of *John Wick* was interrupted by Chan slamming the door open and walking in with a Costco box filled with groceries.

"Ew, what's that smell?" asked Chan.

"Someone left eggshells in the compost bin," said Alex, in a passive-aggressive tone. Alex, when annoyed, can be a dick. But he had good reason to be. Chan made our house smell like shit. Chan was an ass. And shit comes from an ass, and asses apparently can't pick up on passive-aggressive behavior. Alex's remarks did not register with Chan.

While Chan unloaded his groceries, I asked him about his break.

"How was your winter break?" I asked.

"Pretty good. I was sick for most of it, though," he answered.

"Oh, that's a bummer," I said.

"Yeah. My brother had a shit virus," he told us.

"A shit virus?" asked Alex.

"Yeah. We share a toilet, so I got it too," said Chan.

A shit virus? "For our sake, I hope you're feeling better," I said.

"Yup. I'm better now," he replied.

The next day was the first day of the spring semester. It was a Thursday, and I only had one class. Unfortunately, it was a three-hour night class. Per usual, I showed up early. The classroom was empty, so I took a seat. As I browsed Instagram, people started to trickle in. My department was small, so I often had numerous classes with the same people. I was bound to see a familiar face, and I did. A stunning blonde girl named Ash walked in. I'd had a class with her before. She had golden blonde hair and ocean blue eyes, with sun-kissed skin.

I didn't really get the opportunity or have the courage to talk to her in our class the previous semester. That would change. I wanted to make an effort this semester and at least talk to her. All of a sudden, another gorgeous girl entered the classroom. She looked like Sandy at the end of *Grease*. She had platinum blonde hair (not natural), wore black jeans and a black leather jacket, and black boots, like a sexy cat burglar. She put out an Avril Lavigne vibe. The type of vibe where, if you handed her a guitar, she could play it. I was drawn to her right away; she looked a lot like Emily Blunt. If she had an accent like Emily Blunt, I would lose my shit. I love accents. I got the feeling this would become my new favorite class.

We spent the class introducing ourselves and telling the class about our interests.

"Hi, I'm Sheryl," said the girl to my left. "I'm married, I enjoy painting, and during the day I work as an art teacher."

The professor asked her a few follow-up questions. This professor was pushy, but in a positive way. She always tried to get you to give your best.

"Hi, my name is Ash and I'm a dance major, and I'm minoring in creative arts. I love animals, particularly horses. My family actually owns a couple horses. I want to eventually become a teacher."

The professor had a lot of follow up questions, mainly about the horses. They both had a love for horses. Just then, Robbie walked through the door.

I'd had classes with Robbie before. He's a really nice dude, who is not bad looking. With that being said, he had likely diminished any chance I had with these two beautiful girls. Robbie apologized for being late and then took a seat. *Goddammit*, I thought, *this guy is good looking, friendly, and is fashionably late.* I had no shot. To make matters worse, it was now my turn to introduce myself to the class.

"Hi, my name is Nick. I'm not sure what I want to do after college. In my spare time, I like to hang out with my roommate Alex. We've been friends since high school. I love Netflix. I can get lost on there for hours. I also like listening to podcasts, and lately I have been recording a podcast with my friends."

"What is your podcast about?" asked the professor.

"Um, it's just my roommates interacting with a character I play."

"Tell us more, about this character?" she asked, while clicking open her pen.

"The podcast is pretty much random conversations, but I play a character named Gilbert Sanderson, who is an inventor and entrepreneur, who comes on the show and pitches ideas or inventions to people on the podcast. Kinda like *Shark Tank*, but Gilbert's inventions are always awful."

"Inventions?" asked the professor, jotting down some notes.

"Yeah, like his skin exfoliator called Sandpaper Lotion. It's exactly how it sounds."

"Hmm," said the professor, scribbling in her leather-bound notepad. "Tell us more about this Gil character."

"I imagine Gil to be fifty years old and he sounds like Robert Durst. You guys know who Robert Durst is?" Nobody responded. Not even the crickets in a bush outside the window. It feels horrible when a whole class has no idea what you're referencing. To try to salvage this situation, I said, "Check out the docuseries *The Jinx* on HBO. It's pretty good."

"Can we hear him?" asked the professor.

"Who? Gil?" She nodded her head. During this whole exercise, I felt like I was being psychoanalyzed in front of the entire class.

I took a deep breath before I unleashed Gil upon the classroom. Hopefully Ash and Emily Blunt were into improv. I hunched my shoulders up, held my hands up like a T-rex, and lowered my head, trying to look as frail as possible. I then squinted my eyes and said in a raspy, deep voice, "Hi, hello, the name's Gilbert Sanderson, but you can call me Ole Gil."

Everyone in the class was smiling.

"Is the character a New Yorker?" asked the professor.

"Sure," I said confidently. I sat back down, hoping to have made an impression, good or bad. I'm usually invisible in the classroom. I wanted to make a real effort to be more involved and noticeable.

"Hold on, Nick," said the professor, scribbling in her notepad. "Where can we find your podcast? I'm sure some people might want to check it out," she said.

"I recently made a YouTube page where I have been posting. Just go on YouTube and search 'Uhh Wut What?! Podcast'." The professor had me write it on the board so my classmates could write it down. I checked my view count religiously for months and there was no change. Nobody from my class checked it out.

After I sat down, the guy fidgeting next to me began clearing his throat, preparing to speak. By fidgeting, I mean he had been bobbing his knee up and down since the beginning of class. Granted, I was impressed by his display of endurance and leg strength. It was incredibly distracting. It reminded me of a jockey bouncing up and down at the Kentucky Derby.

"Hi, I'm Dan, and I like to draw." Dan went on to tell the class how he loves animation, drawing, and creating his own characters. *We get it, you like making cartoons*, I thought. *Sit down already so I can get some intel on Rock of Ages Emily Blunt.*

Finally, it was Ms. Blunt's turn to speak.

"Hi, everyone. My name is Kimberley, and this is my second semester at SJSU. I'm a music teacher. I teach kids to play guitar, clarinet, and piano. I also perform music. That's pretty much it. I'm kinda basic. Are there any questions?"

"Where do you perform?" asked the professor, writing in her notepad.

"Mainly in Campbell. It's where I live and work."

"Oh, okay," said the professor, nodding. "That's like, what, a fifteen-minute commute from here?" she asked.

"Yeah, but if there is traffic, it ends up being twenty to thirty minutes," she explained.

"Well, let your classmates know if you have any upcoming performances. I'm sure your classmates would love to support you and the arts. After all, this is a senior seminar for creative arts majors. That's kinda what it's all about."

"Well, I do have a YouTube where I post myself doing covers," she told us.

"Oh, that's perfect. If you don't mind, can you write the name of your YouTube channel on the board so we can check it out?" the professor asked.

"Sure," she responded.

The girls in this class were amazing. The aspiring teacher and dancer, Ash. Kimberley, who can play multiple instruments. There was so much talent and beauty between the two of these girls. I started to regret mentioning my love of Netflix. Don't get me wrong, I love Netflix, but bragging about watching Netflix may not have been the best way to impress the ladies. Once Kimberley returned to her seat, I made sure to write down her YouTube channel on the back of my notebook. I wasn't sneaky about it. I wanted her to see me writing it, so she would know that I would check out her page.

"Hey, my name's Robbie, but everyone calls me Rob," said the handsome guy sitting next to Kimberley. Robbie was a threat. I had clocked him as one the moment he stepped foot in the class. He was taller than me. He had hair that looked like he just woke up, but he probably spent half an hour styling it that way.

"I'm a senior and I'm also into performing music," announced Robbie, pointing a finger gun at Kimberley. "I'm in a band with my brother and we play pop-rock." He went on to plug his band, blah, blah, blah…I stopped paying attention. I'd had enough. He was into bands and I was into podcasts. He was clearly cooler than me. He's the type of guy that owns multiple leather jackets. Whatever, how dare he make me doubt myself? Geez, the nerve of some people. These girls are too smart to fall for this ruse. So what, if he makes a cooler first impression? I'm playing the long game, Robbie, so game on! You may have won the battle, but not the war, dude!

Class was dismissed and I was packing up my things when I noticed Robbie walk over to Kimberley and say, "Hey, so you're from Campbell?"

"Yeah," she said, zipping up her leather backpack.

Robbie brushed a couple rogue strands of hair from his face.

"Oh, no way, I live in Campbell too," he bragged.

What is happening right now? Is this a meet cute? Is that what's going on here? Is Robbie meet cute-ing Kimberley right in front of me? I purposely dropped a pencil onto the floor so I could eavesdrop more while retrieving the pencil.

"Where you headed?" he asked.

"Parking garage," she told him.

"Which one?" asked Robbie.

"I forgot the name, but it's the one near Sweeney Hall."

"Oh, yeah, that's the south parking garage. I'm parked there too. I'll walk you to your car."

Side by side, they floated out of the room with their backs facing me. *How the fuck did he do that? He just waltzes right up to her, charms her like a snake, and proceeds to walk her to her car.* I was jealous at the smoothness of his operation. Not only did he look smooth, he also looked chivalrous. Lots of students get mugged when walking back to their cars at night. This guy was a pro, and I was an amateur. I walked myself to my bike and rode home feeling less than great. Despite Robbie's swaggerous presence, once a week, this class would be one of my favorite escapes from Chan.

Chapter 15 - Our Trip to Ranch 99

"UGHHCK—UGGGGG—UGHHHH!" coughed Chan from his loft. I rolled over and checked the time on my phone. It was 7 a.m. on Friday, my sleep-in day. Chan was having one of his morning cough attacks. Though, on this particular morning, his cough sounded worse than usual. It was guttural and very unbecoming. I wouldn't be able to sleep with this ruckus, so I got up to use the bathroom. While I was on the toilet, I decided I wanted to scroll through Instagram. That's when I realized I had left my phone on the charger. I sat and contemplated what work needed to be accomplished over the upcoming weekend. Just then, my thought was interrupted by a chirp.

There must be a bird in the tree, I thought. I began to fall back into my state of contemplation when I heard the chirp again. The chirp was faint but loud enough for me to notice it. In my bathroom, there is a tree right outside of the window that birds and squirrels like to frequent. It was quiet. Chan had stopped coughing, and the chirps seemed to disappear. After about a minute of silence, I heard the chirp again. This time the chirp got louder and louder. I listened intently. Then I heard an, "Uh! Uh!"

The noise wasn't a bird. It was our neighbors having sex. I felt helpless. I was stuck on the toilet, forced to listen to my neighbors having morning sex, with no cell phone to save me. After a while, I heard a male groan.

"Ughhhhhh!"

It sounded similar to Chan's phlegmy-sounding cough. Oh, how I wish it was Chan coughing. After the groan, there was no more noise from the other side of the bathroom wall.

Later on that day, after that awkward morning movement, I was downstairs conversing with Chan and Alex. We were making a list of items to get at the grocery store. Chan was campaigning to go to this store called Ranch 99. Alex and I usually patronized our go-to stores. Our go-to stores consisted of Trader Joe's, Safeway, Target, and Costco. Ranch 99 wasn't on the list. Alex and I agreed to go to Ranch 99 and audition it for our go-to list.

We grabbed our wallets and piled into Alex's car. Chan quickly grabbed Alex's auxiliary cord to play music. *Aw great, here we go,* I thought. Chan started playing music and then turned the volume up so people outside the car could hear it too. After every song, he would ask us if we liked it. How do you tell someone their music sounds like shit, nicely? Instead of complimenting the music as a whole, I would compliment an element of the music. So, when Chan would inevitably ask, "You like that song?" I would say, "The beat was unique," or I would say, "I enjoyed the beat they sampled."

After about five songs courtesy of DJ Chan, we arrived at Ranch 99. Chan pushed the cart and Alex and I trailed behind him.

My initial thought upon entering Ranch 99 was that it overwhelmingly smelled like fish. At that moment, I knew I wouldn't purchase anything from the store, and I knew Alex wouldn't either. Chan is a slow shopper, which is especially frustrating when he has a list written out. He will put an item in the cart and then decide five minutes later that he doesn't want it.

"Are you guys gonna get anything?" asked Chan, noticing that Alex and I hadn't added any items to the cart.

"Nah," I told him.

"I'm good," said Alex. Not only did everything smell like fish, almost everything was written in languages other than English. Alex and I were in the produce aisle watching Chan grope veggies and then put them in the cart. Moments later, he'd replace the veggie that he put in the cart with a more satisfying veggie. Alex and I had fun playing with a jackfruit. We pretended it was an alien egg. Then it turned into a ball, and then a baby. Meanwhile, Chan continued to put veggies in the cart.

"Aren't you going to put those in a bag?" questioned Alex, pointing out that Chan had just put all the vegetables directly into the cart.

"No," said Chan shaking his head. "Why would I do that? They're going to be washed anyway. You guys ready?" asked Chan.

"Yes!" exclaimed Alex.

Alex and I followed Chan, who led the way out of the produce aisle. We stayed close so we wouldn't get lost. After all, this was Chan's turf and he knew the terrain. As we were making our way to the cash register, Chan's cart began to veer right. It veered so much that he crashed it into an aisle. Luckily, nothing fell over. Chan quickly snapped his head back at us with the flexibility of an urban pigeon and spoke:

"Sorry, I was staring at that girl's ass."

Then, he whipped his head around and continued toward the checkout like nothing had happened. Alex and I looked at each other. I rolled my eyes, and Alex grabbed a weird-looking vegetable out of the cart and mimed putting a gun to his head and pulling the trigger. I laughed and then whispered, "Good prop work."

Chan unloaded his cart onto the conveyor belt at the cash register, including his bagless vegetables. The cashier was an old Asian man in his late hundreds. He reminded me of the sloth in the movie *Zootopia*. He probably shops as slowly as Chan does. Mr. Miyagi didn't speak with his mouth but used his eyebrows to do the talking. His mouth was too busy hanging open. He would make the occasional noise and then do a dance with his eyebrow. Chan seemed to know what he was saying. While Chan was trying to figure out if his card had a chip or not, drool started to slowly creep out of the old man's mouth. It began to pick up in speed and drip down the old man's jaw. The strand of drool began to descend. It reminded me of a spider descending from its web. The strand of drool broke and quickly fell onto Chan's un-bagged vegetables.

When we got out of earshot (not that the old man would have been able to hear us anyway), Alex said, "That was the most disgusting thing I've ever fucking seen."

"And that's why we bag our vegetables!" I exclaimed.

Chapter 16 - SICK

It was Monday and I was lying in bed, listening to a combination of Chan's laughter and music he was blasting loudly. His cough had progressively worsened. It had been bad the previous week when we were at the Chinese market, but today it sounded like he was coughing up a lung. I got up and opened the door that connected my room to his loft.

"Morning," I said, giving Chan a nod.

"Morning," said Chan, watching videos on his phone while also listening to music on his computer.

I walked down to the kitchen to make some coffee. I noticed Alex was awake watching *Family Guy* in his room. I went into Alex's room to hang out and sip my morning coffee.

"You hear him coughing?" I asked, gesturing my pointer finger up and down.

"Yeah," said Alex, grinning, "the whole neighborhood probably heard him."

"His cough sounds so phlegmy and sickly," I said.

"Yeah, he's gross," said Alex.

Just then, we heard some thuds. It was Chan, stirring. I heard the video on his phone get louder and louder; he was coming down the stairs. He went into the bathroom connected to Alex's room. We could hear a lot of sounds. We heard him pushing and grunting, accompanied by the sound from the video on his phone. He was shitting. I didn't drink my coffee during this time. All of a sudden, we heard a flush begin and then the door open. We waited for Chan to thump his way back up the stairs to his lair before we spoke.

"He didn't wash his hands," said Alex with a stank face. "He was outta there before the toilet finished flushing."

"What's worse is that there was no wipe time," I said.

Alex started pretending to throw up. Alex was interrupted by Chan hocking up phlegm.

"No wonder he's sick," I said. "The guy doesn't wash his hands."

I went upstairs to change. As I entered Chan's loft, I saw him sitting at his computer.

"Are you sick?" I asked. "You have been coughing a lot lately."

"No, I think it's just allergies," replied a nonchalant Chan.

"Alright, I'ma get ready for school. Hope you feel better."

I got to school early (like usual). As I sat at my desk, waiting for class to start, other students poured in. Some people I recognized but most of my classmates were new to me. In walked in Emily Blunt (Kimberley). She sat down ten seats from me. Clearly, she hadn't noticed me. During the whole class, I would nod to whatever the teacher said and pretend to take copious notes, on the off chance that if she glanced over and noticed me, it would look like I was an intelligent student. This was an exhausting strategy. After class, I purposely packed my bag slowly. This was one of my classic strategies, with a very unsuccessful success rate. By that, I mean it had never worked, until today.

Unfortunately, Kimberley, to my surprise, did notice me. I say "unfortunately" because I was not prepared for my strategy to work.

"Hey," she said, giving me a little wave.

"Hey! Kimberley, right? You're in my senior sem class?" I asked, even though I knew the answers to both questions.

"Yeah. Did you do the reading for senior sem?" *Man, this is going uncomfortably well. I'm not prepared for this. She asked you a question, Nick, you should probably answer her.*

"Not yet. I'll probably do the reading tonight," I said.

"I'm going to have to get it done on Wednesday. I've got a heavy work schedule all week," she told me.

"Well, you've plenty of time," I said.

"Well, see you later," she said.

"See ya," I said and smiled. She walked off. I waved, even though she would never see it. *That was an interesting exchange*, I thought. *Glad I remembered to put on deodorant today.*

The next couple of days, Chan's condition had become a problem. It wasn't "just allergies." He was sick and coughing everywhere. I asked him again if he was sick to see if his answer would change from "just allergies," and it did. His answer this time was:

"It's just the flu."

I answered him with, "People die from the flu." Chan continued to cough. This was a problem, because he does not cover his mouth when he coughs. Since he cooks a lot, he coughs in the kitchen quite a bit. Alex and I went to Target to get some supplies. I picked up some Lysol disinfecting spray.

"I'm not getting sick because he doesn't know how to cover his mouth," I said, putting the spray in the cart. Alex and I then went to the toy section to check out the Nerf guns. While we were there, we noticed a suspicious guy crouched over, looking through a hole in the shelf.

Is this guy some sort of pervert? I thought. *What's he looking at?* I walked past him, pretending to shop while trying to figure out what this pedo next to the Barbie section was peeping at. As I walked by him, I noticed he had an earpiece and was communicating to someone. On the other side of the toy aisle was the electronics section. Clearly, this was a loss protection officer watching a shoplifter. Alex and I continued our shopping.

"You see his handcuffs?" asked Alex.

"No, why?" I said.

"They looked cool. They were matte black," he explained.

"That is cool," I agreed. As we shopped, we saw the officer crouching around the store, spying on the shoplifter. Alex and I were getting a kick out of seeing the shoplifter in the store and then seeing the officer trail behind him like a ninja (or a pervert; both are applicable).

As we were making our way to the checkout, I noticed the shoplifter walking toward us. I gave Alex a nudge to draw his attention to the criminal ahead. As the thief passed by, he gave us a friendly nod.

"Please tell me you didn't nod back," I said to Alex.

"Why?" he questioned.

"Because they will think we're working with him! They will think we're accomplices!" I explained.

"Well, lucky for you, I didn't nod back," said Alex.

"Lucky for us," I said. "If I'm going down, I'm taking you with me."

The shoplifter really looked suspicious. If you told me to point out the shoplifter in the store, I would say, "That guy!" The shoplifter was a white male dressed in black, with a backpack. He wore a bandana that was being covered by a crooked baseball cap. The face tattoo didn't help, either. The tattoo might as well have said, "I did it, cuff me."

Alex and I were standing in line when we noticed the bandana bandit heading for the door. We also spotted the loss protection officer watching him from afar. The bandit slowly walked toward the theft detectors at the store exit. He paced around for a moment, then walked through. The alarm went off instantly. I glanced over at the loss protection officer. I saw him say something to his earpiece, and then he went running over to the bandit.

"Sir, please come here!" he yelled.

"I don't got nothing!" the shoplifter said, walking toward the door.

"Sir, please come with me so we can talk about this," said the officer, putting his hand on the bandit's shoulder.

"Get your hands off me!" he yelled, then sprinted out the door, where he was walled off by a large black man who was waiting for him.

"Get your hands off me! I didn't do anything!" protested the bandit. "This is assault!" he yelled. They escorted him into a room near the front of the store. As Alex and I exited the store, a police car pulled up in front. Alex and I were filled with excitement. This was like watching a live version of *Cops*. Except our perp wasn't wearing jean shorts, which leads me to believe that he was probably an innocent man.

The next morning, I woke up with a scratchy throat, a runny nose, and a bad attitude. Despite my action in spraying down the apartment with Lysol, my effort proved futile. Chan had gotten me sick. I walked downstairs to see if Alex could take me to the store to get some medicine. I walked into his room and found him, lying in bed, watching *Family Guy*. He was also feeling sick and was planning on getting medicine.

Congratulations, Chan, you got the whole house sick.

Alex and I found ourselves back at Target. We bought cough drops, Dayquil, Nyquil, Flonase, tea, honey, and soup. I should have sent Chan the bill for all of this stuff. Luckily, it was Friday, so I could spend a couple of days in bed. The irony of this whole situation was that Chan was better the day Alex and I fell ill. It was as if the sickness had literally moved on from one host to another. Kinda like in *The Exorcist*, where the demon moves from Regan into the priest. Except I was too exhausted to jump out a window.

On Saturday, I was at my worst. I was lethargic, dizzy, feverish, and I had the chills. I was a mess, and I was alone. Alex had gone back home for the weekend, and Chan was getting ready to embark on his soup crusade. He offered me some of the soup he was going to give away to the homeless. I wasn't sure if this gesture was because he felt bad about getting me sick, or because I looked like a homeless person and he couldn't tell the difference. I accepted his soup, complimented it, and thanked him. You see, Chan is not a bad person, he's just an oblivious idiot who may have given me "just the flu."

Chapter 17 - Backdraft

It was Thursday evening. I arrived at my senior seminar night class. I had been looking forward to this class all week; I was excited and a little bit nervous to see Ash and Kimberley. I liked both these girls and looked forward to getting to know them. It's kind of like *The Bachelor*, if the ladies showed little to no interest in him.

I was an hour early to class. The hallway was empty and the classroom was dark. Not wanting to sit in an empty classroom, I sat in the hallway and listened to music on my phone. Out of the corner of my eye, I saw a shadowy figure. *Great, the hallway is haunted*, I thought. After a long, internal motivational speech about facing my fears, I was ready to confront this shadowy apparition. I took a deep breath and turned my head. The shadowy figure wasn't an apparition at all. It was Kimberley. She was wearing all black workout gear, with white high-top shoes. She walked by, gave me a wave, peeked inside the class, and then sat next to me in the hallway.

Is this real life? I asked myself. I began to get nervous and sweaty. Pretty girls have this effect on me. I would have preferred the apparition. That way, my undershirt would have stayed dry.

"Hey," said Kimberley, pulling her MacBook out of her backpack.

I paused my music and then said, "Hello. You're here early."

"Yeah. So are you," said Kimberley, smiling.

"We have similar class schedules," I said. "We have this class and the one with Dr. Richards."

"Yeah, I love Dr. Richards. She's one of the best professors I've had," exclaimed Kimberley.

"She's great," I said, trying to keep the conversation going.

"You look familiar," she said, looking into my eyes.

"Really?" I asked, staring back into hers.

"Yeah, I feel like I've met you before. Or seen you," she explained.

"I mean, we go to the same school so maybe you've seen me around campus?" I offered.

"No, I commute here, so I'm rarely on campus," she said.

"Maybe I just have one of those faces?" I asked.

"Hmm, maybe," she said, moving her hair out of her face. "You transferred here, right?"

"Yeah," I said while nodding my head.

"Me too. So, I think I probably saw you at the transfer student orientation thing. You know, the one that was held in the fall?" she said.

"Oh, yeah, that's probably it," I said.

I didn't go to the fall orientation, I went to the one in the spring. I don't know why I didn't correct her. Maybe I wanted to spend the rare one-on-one time trying to get to know her, and class was going to start soon. This was a race against the clock—a race I wanted to place in.

Unfortunately, other students arrived and joined us in the hallway. My time with Kimberley was over. I just wanted to make a positive impression. I wanted her to think, *That Nick fella is a pretty nice guy, whom I won't friendzone.*

In class, we were assigned a group project. The small class was split into three groups of five. Each group would have to present on five chapters of our assigned reading book. As the teacher was making groups at random, I was praying that I would be in a group with Ash and/or Kimberley. My prayers were answered: I was placed in a group with Ash. After class, we were told to get the contact information of our group members.

"Who is Ash?" said Jessica, trying to find her group members.

"Oh, that's me," responded Ash while putting her hand up.

"Hey, I'm in your group," said Jessica.

"That's great," replied Ash.

"Yeah, it's pretty much the best group ever," I said.

Jessica walked over and took down our contact info. I was thrilled that night as I rode my bike home. I got to have a nice conversation with Kim and group work with Ash.

It was Friday and I didn't have class. Neither did Alex, Drew, or Chan. We decided to have a guys' day out. Chan made breakfast in the morning and then we all suited up for basketball. None of us are any good, which is what makes it a fair game. It was during this low-point-scoring game when we realized Chan may be a superhero.

The teams were Alex and Drew versus Chan and me. If Chan and Drew were on a team, they would have had a huge height advantage. I'll remind you that Chan is six-foot-five and Drew is six-foot-three. Alex and I are both under five-foot-ten. Drew was guarding Chan, and with one arm, Chan would simply push Drew out of the way. Now, with his path to the rim clear, he was wide open. But Chan is no Steph Curry. He would miss and rebound in rapid succession until the ball would seemingly and reluctantly roll in.

"Tenth time's the charm," I joked after Chan scored. Chan was guarding Drew very aggressively. I mean, he was all over him. Thank God he was on my team. I would hate for his sweaty, schlubby body to be that close to my face.

In one crossover move performed by Drew, Chan fell to the ground. It was as if he had been sniped. Drew had broken Chan's ankles.

Okay, he didn't actually break Chan's ankles, but he had definitely broken Chan's spirit and dignity. As Chan flew to

Spilled Curry

the ground, Alex and I turned around and cuffed our mouths to contain the laughter. After I got myself under control, I walked over to make sure Chan was okay. His shin was scraped, and he wanted to walk back to the apartment for a bandage and water. We decide to take a ten-minute break.

Chan never returned. When we arrived back at the apartment, Alex called up to Chan, "Hey, you never came back!"

"Yeah, sorry," said Chan in a somber voice. "I didn't feel up to it."

"Oh, well, we are going swimming if you'd like to join us," I said.

"I'm probably just going to stay in," Chan answered.

"Alright, that's fine. Just thought I would extend you an invitation." I was glad he wasn't going to join us.

Last time we went to the pool, he grossed me out. As we were leaving the pool, Alex was joking around and pointed out the pool rules to Chan—one rule in particular. The rule was something along the lines of, "Do not use the pool if you have had diarrhea within the last fourteen days." Alex was implying that Chan had diarrhea. Hah-hah. Alex isn't the best observational humorist, but I applaud his effort.

After Chan read the sign, he looked at Alex and said, "Too late."

We all laughed.

"Good one," Drew said.

"I'm being serious," said Chan.

"When did you have diarrhea? Was it when you were sick a couple weeks ago?" Drew asked.

"I had diarrhea today."

"What?" asked a serious and fearful Alex.

"You're fine. The chlorine kills all the germs," said Chan.

We walked back to the apartment in silence. Later, Chan was in the shower, Drew was out back smoking, and Alex and I used this time to talk some shit.

"Oh my God, he's fucking disgusting," said Alex.

"He's gross! And, thanks to him, now I'm gross. I swam around in his fecal-matter pool water. What makes this situation worse is that you know he doesn't wipe!" I gagged. This unfortunate memory made me cringe.

Alex, Drew, and I enjoyed our guys' day out at the pool. I noticed Alex was putting on some sunscreen, which reminded me to put some on.

"Hey, can I borrow some of your sunscreen?" I asked.

Alex tossed the tube over to me and I didn't catch it because it was all slippery from the sunscreen. Hopefully, none of the girls sunbathing noticed this lapse in reflexes. I used my towel to wipe down the tube, and that's when I noticed that this was not sunscreen.

"Alex, this is not sunscreen," I said, holding up the tube. "It's suntan lotion."

"Same thing!" retorted Alex.

"It's not. This is like fifteen SPF and I don't wear anything under seventy SPF. Everybody knows that," I said.

"Psht!" puffed Alex. "Does it even matter?"

"It's fifteen SPF!" I roared. "Might as well cover yourself with butter!" Since these were dire times, I figured that the suntan lotion was better than nothing. When I entered the pool, I was a caramel complexion, and when I exited the pool, I looked like tech support. I had turned fifty shades darker, and I hold a tan for an unbelievable amount of time. I'm often mistaken for being Indian or Middle Eastern during the summer months.

My brown complexion once got me into a frustrating situation. A year earlier, I was at a taqueria, waiting with Alex and Drew for our order of burritos. As we were waiting, I noticed a heavyset Latino man staring at me. I began to try to analyze what he could be looking at. *Do I look like someone he knows? What could it be?* I thought. Then it hit me. I was standing in front of a window; there must have been something going on behind me. *That's gotta be it*, I thought, reassuring myself. Case closed. During this analyzation, the Latino man's friend went to the counter and got their food. The Latino man walked up to me and said, "Why do you look like a Middle Eastern faggot?"

I was confused about what the Latino man had just said. All I could say in response was, "I'm not."

He was wrong on both counts. I'm not Middle Eastern and I'm not gay. The whole thing was very confusing. I was trying to figure out the connection between being Middle Eastern and being gay. I'm brown skinned, with a Latino ethnic background, same as his. The gay comment? I was wearing my workout gear. Perhaps he assumed I was gay because I'm in shape and well groomed? Not to mention, he made a racist comment in the form of a question.

As I said, it was very confusing. With all these thoughts running through my head, I heard him say it again:

"Why do you look like a Middle Eastern faggot?"

As he said this, he pounded his fist into his palm. You know, like bullies do in movies, right after they ask for your lunch money?

Again, I answered with, "I'm not." My mind was rapidly processing what was happening, and running through scenarios of what was going to happen. *Am I going to fight? What if I get kicked out from school? What will my parents think?* But before anything happened, his friend returned with their order and shepherded him out the door.

"Sorry that happened to you," said Drew.

"He was just drunk," said Alex.

"He was?" I asked.

"Yeah, don't you see him all hunched over and swaying?" Alex explained. I had just thought he had bad posture. I glanced out of the window, looking at the drunk, racist Latino man as he stumbled across the street, miming fighting me. I felt sad, not for myself, but for people who are Middle Eastern and regularly endure racism like that.

Back at the pool, Alex, Drew, and I were sitting on our towels, all looking at our phones. Alex was Snapchatting girls, and Drew was looking at local marijuana delivery services. I noticed Ash had written in my group chat about meeting up at the library later that week. I responded promptly to the invitation.

Later that evening, as things were winding down, Chan was up in his loft playing computer games while Alex and I watched some *Flip or Flop*. During the show, a flicker of light caught the corner of my eye. I turned my head and saw a flame in the toaster oven. I stood up and asked Alex, "Are you cooking something in the toaster oven?"

He answered with, "No, why?"

"'Cause something is on fire," I said.

We rushed over to the toaster oven. We couldn't see what was in it because of the smoke.

Alex yelled up to Chan, "HEY, CHAN! YOUR DINNER IS ON FIRE!"

"Okay!" responded Chan.

"YOUR FOOD IS LITERALLY ON FIRE!"

We then heard loud rumbling. It was either an avalanche or Chan rushing down the stairs. Chan quickly opened the door to the smoky toaster oven. The smoke bellowed out, revealing a whole chicken covered in oil that Chan had attempted to cook in the toaster oven.

Chan began to panic. He frantically began to shout, "What do I do? What do I do? What do I do?"

"Grab some oven mitts and put it in the sink!" I yelled.

But that was too logical. Instead, Chan took a deep breath and blew into the toaster oven in an effort to extinguish the small flame. It was evident Chan had never seen the film *Backdraft*. Chan blowing into the toaster oven just fed the flame. There was a flash—the flame had combusted into an *Inferno*! (Another film Chan has probably not seen.)

The kitchen was cast with a warm orange glow. As the flames began to creep out of the toaster oven, I watched the billowing smoke start to stain the cabinets above black, like spilled ink on parchment.

"Do something, Chan!" I yelled.

"What should I do?" he shrieked. I was worried that the cabinets above the toaster oven would catch fire and then spread to the rest of the apartment.

"Well, put the oven mitts on and move it from underneath the cabinets," I offered. Maybe it was the smoke, but I began to envision standing in front of our apartment building, wrapped in blanket and watching the fire department try to extinguish our scorched building. I didn't want to be the guy whose apartment burned everyone else's apartment into ash. Even if it wasn't my fault, just being associated with the apartment would suck. Let's be honest, burning down the apartment building just isn't a good look, very hard to pull off.

I snapped into reality when Alex yelled, "You gonna do something, or what?"

Chan was freaking out. Actually, we were all freaking out. I stared at Chan, waiting for him to take action. As I stared, I was processing possible ways to solve this escalating situation. *If he's not going to do something, then I will.* In my mind, I had come up with a solution. My idea was that the stainless steel sink would be able to house the flaming pan of chicken and allow us to easily spray it with water and put out the fire. Before I could put my plan into action, I saw a wave of transformation take place. I saw Chan go from looking clueless, as usual, to looking very focused. That's when he sprang into action. He quickly grabbed a hand towel and draped it over his hands. Then, without hesitation, he reached into the toaster oven for the flaming pan of chicken. So far, he was following the plan I had come up with. Except, I would have grabbed the oven mitts. I decided to vocalize the rest of my plan to Chan:

"Throw it in the sink!" I yelled.

A heroic-looking Chan pulled out the flaming pan of chicken and turned toward us. Chan did not heed my advice, and like Elsa, he let it go. He dropped the flaming pan on the kitchen floor! The fire, to my surprise, was extinguished the moment the chicken splatted against the floor. After a brief silence from the chaos, Chef Chan looked up from the floor and told us, "Sorry, I didn't know you couldn't cook a chicken in a toaster oven. I'll clean this up."

I could see how his chicken had caught on fire. As he mopped up the mess, I noticed a large amount of olive oil was smeared across the floor. Oil? Heat? A confined space? Come on, dude. I hope Chan learned a valuable lesson about trying to cook a whole chicken in a toaster oven that day, or at least a lesson in science.

Chapter 18 - Mama Chan

It was a Thursday evening and I was riding my bike through the streets of San Jose, on my way to the library. I was going to my second group meeting for my senior sem project. The previous one went very well. We had a very productive meeting full of ideas and creativity. During the meeting, Ash and I were on the same page. We were creatively on the same wavelength. I would pitch an idea and she would like it. Then she would pitch an idea and I would like that. We were vibing the whole meeting. After that meeting, I walked Ash to her car like a goddamn gentleman. I got the feeling that she liked me back. I was very eager for this upcoming second group meeting, to try to win her over.

I found Ash sitting in one of the aisles outside of our conference room. The library at our school has conference rooms bordering the book aisles. It's a great place to study and converse with people. She was sitting on the floor in the geography section, reading the assigned book for class. As I quietly approached, all I kept thinking was, *Be cool, man*. Oh, and I quietly approached because I was in a library, not because I was trying to creep.

"Hey, Ash," I said, giving her a casual wave in a very friendly, non-creepy way. "How are you?"

"Good, just waiting for them to finish up," she said, pointing to a couple of students who had booked the time slot for the room before us.

I grabbed a book off the shelf called *Minerals and You*. "This seems like an exciting read," I said, pointing out the title to Ash. She flashed a smile. "How much of the assigned reading have you read so far?" I asked.

"I've read most of it. I didn't read as much as I would have liked to because my grandma was in town," she explained.

"Is your grandma against reading?" I joked.

"Oh no, she's just a bit of a handful and requires attention," Ash said.

"Oh, one of those kinds of grandmas? I can relate," I said.

"You have a kooky grandma too?" she asked.

"I had a grandma like that. She passed last semester," I responded.

"Oh, I'm sorry for your loss," said Ash.

"It's fine. We knew it was going to happen. Cancer," I said, making a face. "So, why does your grandma require attention?" I said, trying lift the mood.

"She just does and says things that are vulgar," Ash said.

"Like what?" I, of course, asked.

"For instance, last Christmas, my grandma was talking to my boyfriend about her underwear. So embarrassing. She's quite the character," she said, chuckling.

Boyfriend? Had she just peppered that in like I wouldn't notice? *NOOOOOOOOOOOO! Why? I thought we really hit it off. Did that time where I shared about my grandma passing mean nothing to her?* Clearly, I had misread the situation. All the little cute moments were apparently not moments at all. Once, before class, we had sat together and watched an old video of Robin Williams doing stand-up. How cool is that? I had been sure she was going to be my future ex-wife. She checked all the boxes. She was very outgoing, gorgeous, laughed at my stupid jokes, and didn't seem to mind that I was shy and had awkward tendencies. I guess it just wasn't meant to be. When it comes to reading girls, I'm dyslexic.

"My grandma was pretty crazy too," I said, trying to cope with this sad, unfortunate reality.

"How so?" asked a beaming Ash.

"Once, for Christmas, my grandma gave me a bunch of box cutters."

"That's not too bad," she said.

"I was seven," I added.

"Oh, yikes. That's pretty bad," said Ash.

"Yeah, I don't know why a seven-year-old would need ten box cutters," I said jokingly.

She smiled and shrugged her shoulder, and then glanced over to the conference room. "It looks like they are finishing up with the conference room," said Ash, as she gathered her things. Our second meeting went well, and I got over the news of Ash's boyfriend. In the immortal words of Jay-Z, I was "on to the next one." Hopefully, the next one would be Kimberley. I got along with Kimberley and often talked to her before class, but with my luck, she probably had a boyfriend too.

The next morning, Drew, Alex, Chan, and I were going to go play some basketball. "You ready, Chan?" yelled Alex.

"Yeah, hold on, I'm trying to order my hat!!" yelled Chan from his loft.

"What hat?" yelled Alex.

"My MAGA hat!" Chan answered.

"Your *what* hat?" Alex asked. I turned the TV off so these two lunatics could hear each other and stop shout-talking.

"My Make America Great Again hat." (Cue eyeroll.)

"Well, hurry already," said an impatient and annoyed Alex.

"One sec, I'm almost done. Just gotta place the order." We then heard some vigorous clicking. The clicking stopped and Chan popped his head over the loft ledge and spoke in a monotone.

"Whelp, my computer is frozen." He paused as if he were waiting for a response from the group, but we just stared impatiently back at him. We didn't care about his computer, we just wanted to play some ball. "I'll deal with this later. Let's just go," said Chan.

"Finally," muttered Alex under his breath.

Our time on the court was cut short by Drew breaking Chan's ankles for a second time. We were about ten minutes into our game when I saw Chan go flying to the ground. It was one of the most un-graceful acts of human movement I have ever seen. It was like he had fallen and hit the ground before he actually made any contact with the ground. He was a little shaken up, and was understandably not in the mood to play anymore. You would think he would play in better shoes. He had a pair of old, worn-out Nikes that he liked to wear. I know he has other sports shoes with better grip. I know this because he has a plastic storage container filled with shoes in our hallway closet, not to mention all the shoes he keeps sprawled throughout the living room.

Back at the apartment, everyone but Chan was downstairs watching *Tosh.0*. Chan strolled into the living room looking concerned.

"You okay, dude?" asked Drew, prepping the bong.

"Not really," said Chan.

"Still sore from earlier? It's not something that a little weed can't fix," chuckled Drew, waving the bong.

"It's not that, it's just that I accidentally ordered six Make America Great Again hats," Chan told.

"What the fuck?" Drew laughed.

I interrupted, "What? How did that happen?"

"When I clicked the 'place order' button, the computer froze. So, I clicked it a bunch of times and ended up ordering six hats on accident," he said in a disappointed tone.

"Fail!" said Alex.

"Why don't you just return 'em?" asked Drew.

"I'm not sure if I can get a return, since sales are donations toward the campaign," he said.

"Oh," I said. "Yeah, that might be an issue."

"Yeah, I don't know what to do," Chan said.

"Just send an email," I said. "Explain your situation, and hopefully they understand."

"Kay," said a somber Chan.

We all found the whole hat-tastrophe amusing. He had spent over one hundred dollars on MAGA hats and wanted a refund of his donation.

The next evening, I was home enjoying the house to myself. The other guys were home visiting. Days like these were my most productive. I would get all my work done, then enjoy the amenities of our apartment. I had just sat down to watch the Warriors game when the living room door flung open. Chan stampeded in, along with some of his family members.

"Oh, hey," said Chan, bringing a Costco box full of food into the kitchen. Following behind Chan was his dad (the one that "gave" me the ethernet cord), his mom, and his brother.

I stood up and time froze. I began to contemplate what measure of decorum to proceed with. Should I bow? Would that be received as respectful or just racist? I deferred to my normal introductory procedure and said, "Hello," and gave a small wave.

"Hi," said Chan's mom. "I'm Wing." Wing? *That's an unusual name*, I thought. *I've never met a Wing before.* Chan's mom looked a lot like him. They had the same mouth. Like, exactly the same.

Chan, his dad, and his brother were all in cargo shorts. I was quite amused by this and I began to wonder, *Do they go on father-son shopping sprees and buy the same clothing?* Wearing the same outfit as your dad stops being cute after age three. *Maybe they buy their cargo shorts in bulk?* Then, it hit me. I had an epiphany about something I've often pondered.

Who buys clothes at Costco? I assume it's usually out-of-touch grandmas who don't know what to get their grandkids. Then, the grandkids return the clothes for store credit and get a video game. But other than clueless grandmas, who buys their clothes there? I understand how buying things like socks and underwear in bulk is appealing, but for anything else? I'm not going to wear jeans by the same company who makes my trail mix. So? Well, apparently, the Chans do. They're the type of people who buy their clothes at Costco and in bulk, because Chan has cargo shorts for every day of the week, and I'm assuming his dad and brother do, too. After making some unwanted small talk with the Chans, I returned to watching the game. Chan's dad joined me while Wing, A.K.A. "Mama Chan," helped Chan put away the groceries.

"Whose old bag of celery is this?" asked Chan's mom, holding up the bag. I glanced over to see Chan's mom on her knees with her head inside the fridge while she held out the bag of mushy brown celery.

This should be good, I thought, knowing that Chan was to blame.

"Oh, that's mine," said Chan.

She popped her head out of the fridge and looked over to Chan. "You gotta throw this stuff away," she said in a disappointed tone. "Finish unloading the groceries while I help with these dishes."

"Kay," said Chan, giving her a nod.

"Hey, you guys okay camping out here for a bit? I want to clean these dishes. Why don't you guys watch the game with Nick," said Mama Chan to her kin.

Mama Chan clearly wore the pants in the relationship. Well, in the case of the Chans, she wore the cargo shorts of the relationship. The way she phrased the question made it seem like she was asking them, but her tone was authoritative. She was telling them by asking them.

"Sure," said Chan's dad.

"How long are we going to stay here for?" whined Chan's brother.

"Just watch the game," said Chan's dad. Mama Chan began emptying the dishwasher.

"Where should I put this?" asked Chan's mom, holding a plate.

"Anywhere," said Chan. *Anywhere? I wondered. We have a designated cabinet for dishes, just like we have a designated drawer for utensils. Why would he tell her to put it anywhere? Once again, Chan had left me in awe. Now I'm going to have to reorganize the cabinets after class tomorrow.*

"Oh, that's a cute vase," said Chan's mom, interrupting the Warriors game.

What vase? I thought.

"Can I use it?" she asked, pointing to Alex's boot-shaped glass.

"Uh, it's usually used for drinking out of, but you can you use it," I said, retrieving the glass beer boot. I handed it to Mama Chan, and she placed some spatulas and tongs in it. *I'm sure Alex will be thrilled to see his prized Oktoberfest glass beer boot being used as a kitchen utensil container. Also, if she thinks it's a vase, why is she using as a utensil holder?*

"Who would leave a pot of rice like this on the stove?" complained Mama Chan.

"Oh, that's mine," said Chan.

She gave him a look and then placed the pot with old rice into the sink. I felt like Mama Chan was asking questions to point out messes hoping that it was Alex or me. But every mess she pointed out belonged to her son, Chan.

What a feeling. It felt great to have a mess pointed out to Chan and have him acknowledge it. After she was done with the dishes, she stood in the living room with both hands on her hips. As she stood, she scanned the room like a hawk seeking field mice. Her work was not done. One of the messes in the living room had to be someone else's other than Chan's, right? She was out for blood, or validation that her son wasn't a hot mess.

"Chan, is this pile of clothes yours?" she asked.

Chan quickly peeled himself off the leather couch. As he did so, the couch made a chilling sound, unsticking itself from his shirtless body. Chan walked over to the pile of clothes, against the wall that borders the kitchen to living room. I thought this was a bit redundant, since he was the only one who left his clothes there. The shirt he'd had on moments earlier was at the top of the pile. After glancing down at the pile, he confirmed his mom's suspicions.

"Yeah," answered Chan. "Those are mine."

"Why do you leave your clothes in the living room?" she asked, with a disappointed expression.

"It's just so convenient to take them off and leave them here," explained Chan. *Convenient for you.*

"These should go in your room," she said. *Preach!*

"It's fine," he said, "nobody minds." *Really, dude? Nobody minds? Alex and I have told you multiple times and have physically moved piles of clothing to your room.*

"When are we going to leave?" moaned Chan's brother.

"I'm dealing with your brother right now," snapped Mama Chan.

"I want to go home," demanded Chan's brother.

"Shut it!" barked Chan's dad.

This back and forth of Chan's mom asking about a mess and Chan taking ownership of it went on for five more minutes until his family finally left.

Chan's mom was only here for an hour and a half and has already done more cleaning than Chan since school started. I laughed to myself and got back to my game. As I started to relax, Chan began to watch a Trump speech on very high volume. Ugh...so much for a peaceful day to myself.

Chapter 19 - Presentations

It was the morning of my first group presentation of the spring semester. I was in the kitchen making a of bowl oatmeal when Chan's water pitcher caught my eye. Every time I cleaned the kitchen, I put Chan's water pitcher on top of the fridge because of our limited counter space. The reason I never put it in the fridge is that Chan thinks cold water is bad for you. Here is another classic Chanism. Chan's grandma once told him cold water was bad for him to drink, so he refused to keep his water pitcher in the fridge. Instead, he left it either on the counter or in the sink. That's a ridiculous notion, I know. But to Chan, his grandma's words are golden. Chan is a blind believer in the older and wiser. If Chan's grandma told him breathing through his nose was bad, Chan would solely be a mouth breather.

I remember the exact moment when Chan revealed this cold-water phobia. Alex and I were tired of putting his water away. We asked him why he kept his water pitcher out. Chan said to us, in all seriousness, "My grandma told me that keeping the water in the fridge is bad for you."

I was so baffled by his stupid but sincere response that I responded with an equally sincere response: "Well, that's not true."

"I'm just going to do what my grandma said," said Chan in a soft tone. I learned at an early age that not everything my grandma says is accurate. When I was ten, I was on a vacation with my mom, sister, and grandmother in Los Angeles. We were in a taxi on the way to the hotel. My grandma said in a concerned tone, "I think they found me."

"Who?" I frighteningly asked.

"The paparazzi, they're following us," she explained.

Pop-a-what? I thought. I learned two things that day. I learned what a paparazzo was, and that my grandma was crazy.

I loved my grandma, but she was, on occasion, delusional and a bit inappropriate. Another instance of her proclivity for unbecoming behavior was when I was a small child. She informed me that I was once a fish. Confused would be an understatement. I was a young, dyslexic, impressionable child. Plus, adults are supposed to know everything about anything. *A fish?* I wondered. *What kind of fish? Like a shark? A whale?* She told me that I was a very tiny fish called a sperm. *A sperm fish?* I had never heard of that one before. After learning this fascinating fact about myself, I could not wait to tell everyone how I used to be a sperm fish. That was the last unsupervised visit I had with my grandma.

I know Chan loves his grandma a great deal; he even has a picture of her in his room. He also has a plant that she gave him in his room. Sorry...*had* a plant. The plant had been dead for six months at this point. He still hadn't thrown it away because it was a gift from his grandma. I get he respects and trusts his grandma, but come on, cold water is harmful?

While I waited for my morning coffee to brew and my oatmeal to cool down, I moved Chan's room-temp water pitcher to the top of the fridge. I knew that when I returned, it would be staring at me from the counter. That morning, I arrived to class early and rehearsed with my group. This group project was separate from the one I worked with Ash on for our senior sem class. This particular project was about an artist who used their work as a means to bring attention to an issue or social injustice. All the selected artists shared a theme of being imprisoned for their work and ideologies. Every group was assigned an artist from around the world. The artist we were presenting on was on a Tibetan singer named Lolo. It was my job to dissect the lyrics of the song and talk about its underlying meanings.

Kimberley was in this class and she made me nervous. I had a crush on her. I wanted to impress her with my presentation. I wanted to demonstrate my confidence and knowledge. Some of the pressure was off because she was in the back of the classroom, taking notes on her computer. *Alright.* I told myself. *You got this, Nick. Just pick a spot in the back of the classroom to focus on.* I picked the back of Kimberley's MacBook. That way, everyone would think I was talking at them. In reality, I would be talking past them. Plus, Kimberley's face was hidden behind it. My nerves were settled, and it was game time. Right as I began to present, Kimberley jerked her head to the side of her computer screen and stared me down. She was watching me present, and just like that, we made EYE contact. It threw me off. I began to fumble my words and stutter. It was a disaster. I went from one hundred to zero, real quick. I began to speak while my eyes darted around the room to make it appear like I wasn't purposely looking at her. I was hoping it would seem like my eyes had just happened to land there. As I continued to present, I thought it might be a good idea to check back in on Kimberley to see if she was still looking at me. *Shit!* We made eye contact again. I could tell my group members were disappointed in me. Hell, I was disappointed in me. At the end of our presentation, I complimented my group members by telling them they did a good job. They responded with, "Thanks," not with a, "Thanks, you too."

    Later that week, after my senior sem class, Kimberley, to my surprise, walked up and began talking to me. I was surprised because I hadn't seen her since my horrendous presentation. We chatted about the progress of our upcoming presentations for that class. This somehow led to her telling me that some guy kept stalking her at work. I was nervous and my palms were sweaty, but we were having a normal conversation. In fact, the conversation was going so well that I began critiquing my conversational skill during the conversation. This is something that you should never do. When you doubt yourself, that's when things can take a turn.

    My confidence immediately plummeted. *I hope this conversation doesn't end with a high-five or handshake.* Then I thought, *Why would it end like that? That would be weird, right? Am I giving too much eye contact? Is there such thing as too much eye contact? Should I look away? Her eyes are so pretty, though. It sucks that she's stuck looking at my brown eyes when she's got these blue eyes with notes of green. I should stare at something else.* So, instead of looking into her eyes while I talked with her, as a result of the chaotic critiquing on top of trying to be funny and maintain a conversation, I thought it was a good idea to stare at her teeth. That's right, *her teeth*. After about a minute of hard eye-to-teeth contact, I could see her realize I was staring at her teeth, to which her physical response was to slowly close her mouth for the remainder of the conversation. That obviously put an abrupt end to the conversation entirely.

When I got back to the apartment, Chan and Alex were talking politics. Alex was for Bernie and Chan was for Donald. I remember Alex saying he was never going to win. I remember Chan saying, with great confidence, that not only would Donald Trump win, he was going to build a wall and Make America Great Again. Chan had clearly forgotten that I was Mexican. I didn't want to get in the middle of this ideological, political shit storm. I bit my tongue and went to my room. I'd had a rough week. I just wanted to lay down and watch Netflix until I fell asleep.

All week, I was nervous about seeing Kimberley. Me, nervous? Nothing new; I'm always nervous and awkward. Awkward is my brand. I was just a little more on edge, since I had made things awkward the last time I had seen her. To my benefit, I didn't see Kimberley all week. I assumed she was sick, which would be great; she would probably forget how unslick I was. When you're puking your brains out, you tend to forget minute-long awkward moments with someone you barely know.

A few days later, at my next senior sem project group meeting, things didn't go as smoothly as the ones previously. While we were brainstorming an activity to go along with the overall presentation, one of our group's members walked in almost an hour late. *What is her problem?* I thought. *Shandra was all gung-ho when we first got together as a group, but now she hardly communicates with the group, and now she's late? Ash and I have been the backbone of our group. The rest of our group has been a disappointment. At least they showed up to the meeting on time. Even that fuckboy lady-killer, Robbie, was on time.* I crossed my arms when she walked in, to send a message. Shandra walked in wearing professional-looking garb.

"Can I talk to you guys for a minute?"

This oughta be good, I thought smugly.

It was.

Shandra explained to us that she had not only been unenrolled from the class but also from the university. There had been some discrepancies regarding her student loans and she was two thousand dollars short. So, her enrollment to the class was removed. She was "technically" not a student. Which meant she didn't have access to the school network we used to message each other. This explained the lack of communication on her end. She began to tear up as she told us. This was her third time taking the class. In fact, it was the last class she needed in order to graduate. The class was only offered in the spring, which meant she would have to wait an entire year to retake it. Now think about that: that's four years for one class. Most students are lucky if they get through all of college in four years. The first two times she had taken the class, she had struggled with her thesis. A majority of our grade for the class was our senior thesis (which I'll explain later). Essentially, if you fail that, then it's impossible to pass the class.

The conference room was quiet. Everyone was feeling empathetic and sorry for Shandra. I quickly uncrossed my arms.

I said, "I'm sorry this happened. Is there anyone you can talk to? The bursar's office or a dean or something?"

"I've been trying. It seems like they can't enroll me until next semester. But since this is the only class I need to graduate, it's going to be a year. Fuck! I'm so sick of this bullshit," she said, wiping tears from her eyes. "I just want to be done. I just want to finish school. I wasn't even supposed to be in college."

At the beginning of the semester, when we introduced ourselves to the class, Shandra had shared her story. She used to be homeless, on the streets, struggling to put herself through school. Now she was working, with a roof over head, paying for college. She was amazing. I told Shandra this situation sucks, and that I was sorry she's had so many hurdles in the past. I encouraged her that once she overcame them, the victory would be so much sweeter.

She sighed. "Well, I wanted to tell you guys this in person, and that I'm probably not going to be able to present with y'all next week."

"That's totally fine," said Ash. "Take care of you, girl."

"Well, I'ma go," said Shandra softly.

We all said our goodbyes.

"Good luck. Hope things work out," said Ash in an uplifting tone.

After Shandra left, we got back to work. We had to make the most of the group time, since we all had different schedules. Ash wanted to hear a brief summary of what everyone was going to say about their assigned chapter. To my and her surprise, we were the only ones who had read the chapters.

"Well," I said, trying hard not to sound like a condescending asshole, "try to get the reading done over the weekend and then just message us what you are going to cover in the presentation."

"It's fine. I'm probably going to YOLO it," said Robbie.

My eyes turned red, and in a blind fury, I screamed, "You don't fucking YOLO a presentation, you shitfuck!"

Okay, I didn't say that, I just thought it. In reality, I just pressed my lips together and nodded my head. Seriously, though, if you are going to "YOLO" a presentation, you don't admit it to your group. Our group was already down a member, and now we had Robbie basically saying he was going to half-ass it.

That night, while I was getting ready for bed, I couldn't stop thinking about how lucky and privileged I was to be in college. I, too, was never supposed to be here. My whole life, I struggled through school. I was a brown kid with dyslexia, who would get in trouble for distracting others. Hearing Shandra's situation had humbled me. I reflected on my own journey to be at SJSU. That was the motivational fuel I needed to power through school to the finish line. I messaged Ash and told her I'd pick up the slack, do the reading, and present Shandra's chapter. She felt bad and volunteered to help. So, we both took on the load of Shandra's chapter, along with our own.

A week later was the day of the presentation, and to my surprise, my whole group was early. We got in a good rehearsal, and then it was showtime. Everyone in my group looked presentable. I was in a navy blue button-up shirt with white polka dots. It's formal but friendly. Ash looked great; she had outdone everyone by wearing a blazer. She looked like a news anchor. You know someone's legit if they are wearing a blazer. I once went to a real estate seminar where three speakers all wore the same blazer. By that, I mean there was only one blazer and the three speakers would share it. Once one speaker was done pitching, he would go backstage and give it to the next speaker, and then that speaker would come out with the blazer on. Their co-op blazer fit some of the speakers better than others. I had no idea what they were talking about because I was distracted by whole blazer swap. Apparently, I was the only one bothered by it, because everyone else seemed on board with their pyramid scheme. That was the day I learned the power of the blazer.

Ash is a smart girl. I wasn't surprised she was utilizing the power of the blazer. Ash was the first one of my group members to present. She knocked her presentation out of the park. I was next. I was nervous. Kimberley was sitting in the front row, looking at me. As nice as I looked, I was well aware that she was only looking at me because it was my turn to present and I was the one who was supposed to be talking. After taking a second to get a calm, deep breath in, I was able to regain my composure. This time, I didn't look anywhere near Kimberley. I just picked the wall in the back of the class to look at. This strategy worked. I didn't fumble my words or have an internal panic attack. I managed to give a pretty good presentation. I had also put together a slideshow to compliment the presentation.

After my presentation, it was Robbie's turn. *Let's see this bullshit that Robbie YOLO'd together*, I thought. I had very low expectations. I had seen Robbie adding pictures to the slideshow thirty minutes before we were due to present.

Robbie discussed his assigned chapter, which was about the AIDS epidemic in the 70s and the lack of willingness to help because it was labeled a "gay disease." Surprisingly, I learned a lot from Robbie's presentation. Holy shit, his presentation was not only good, it was great. He impressed everyone—especially our group. At the end of his presentation, he asked, "Any questions?"

That confident S.O.B. If this is him YOLOing, imagine him when he tries. Then, I realized his plan. He had just said that so we would all have low expectations, then when he did a good job, we would think he did a great job. That's too calculated, right? He can't be good looking and a genius, right? Maybe my presentation wasn't as polished because I had to do extra work. Plus, Robbie had the shortest chapter. He had clearly had more prep time than I had. While finding ways to rationalize why Robbie had done such a great job in order to validate my own presentation, I saw Kimberley walking toward me. She looked like she wanted to say something. As she walked up to my desk, I made sure to give myself a friendly reminder to look into her eyes. *Alright, asshole, just look at her eyes and nothing else. Just look at her eyes, man, just look at her eyes. Don't even think about looking at her teeth.* So, I stood there, wide-eyed and staring at her face, as she walked over. Our eyes never met. She walked past me to Robbie. I overheard Kimberley tell Robbie he did a good job. I sighed and thought, *FML.*

It was bad enough that, after class, Kimberley would wait around for Robbie because they parked in the same garage. They used the buddy system and walked together. At least, that's the reason I told myself. It seems suspect. On the other hand, it's smart. People get robbed/accosted frequently late at night in San Jose. Our class let out late. There I go, always rationalizing. I'm not saying something was going on between the two, but it wouldn't have surprised me. Having worked with Robbie, I knew he had a girlfriend. But it wouldn't surprise me to find out he hadn't let Kimberley know that information.

After Kimberley and Robbie chatted for a bit, Robbie was called over to the professor's desk. I was packing my bag during this time. While Kimberley waited for fuckboy Robbie to finish getting praised by the professor for his presentation, she walked over to me and said:

"Hey, how's it going?"

Wow, what is happening right now? My heart raced.

Maybe there is hope, after all, I thought. *See, Nick, you did give a good presentation* (as if being a good presenter in a college class affects whether someone likes you or not). But I was a prisoner of the moment. I tried to sound smooth when I answered, "I'm swell. So, I noticed you were out of class all last week, you alright?"

"Oh, I'm fine. Things just got really busy at work. Then, last weekend, this guy kept following me around the venue." Kimberley was a music teacher and she also often performed music. "He kept calling me because my business is to teach people music and my number is on my business cards."

"That's gross," I said. "Not him liking you, but him pursuing you like that."

"Yeah, I knew what you meant." She laughed.

Come on, Nick, don't insult her intelligence. "So, what happened?" I asked, looking into her eyes.

"Well, he kept, like, following me around. Get this—he tried impressing me by telling me he worked at Startup. Like that's going to make me like you," she said, smiling. "So, I ended up telling my boss about this guy. She quickly banned him from all our events."

"Good for you," I said. And then, it hit me. *Hold up*, I thought. *What is this? What is actually happening right now? She is telling me about guy troubles as if I'm one of her girlfriends. Is she friendzoning me? Oh my God, it's happening. I'm being friendzoned. FUCK MY LIFE!* I thought in a panic. I immediately regressed back to old habits and began staring at her mouth again. To my benefit, Robbie had just finished his chat with the professor and they left together, saving me from any further awkwardness.

To make matters worse, I had to ride home in the dark. I had been so distracted by my preparation for the presentation, I'd forgotten my bike lights. While riding home, all I could think about was how I had witnessed myself get friendzoned by a girl who I really liked. During the dark ride home, I was filled with self-doubt. I began to analyze myself and try to diagnose my issue. *Maybe I'm not cool enough? A leather jacket could really turn this thing around*, I thought. *Note to self, search Amazon for a leather jacket when I get home. Maybe I'm not funny enough? Maybe I'm not tall enough? Maybe I'm not douchey or mean enough?* Once a girl told me that I was "too nice." Like being nice was a bad thing. Comments like that really confuse the psyche. It was a dark, depressing ride home. However, I did have spring break to look forward to. During that spring break, I bought a new leather jacket.

Chapter 20 - Chan Returns! From Spring Break

Our spring break was a week long, but it felt like a day. I guess it's true what they say—time flies when you're having fun. Oh, I forgot to mention, Chan spent his break in San Diego with his computer friends. Alex and I had the place to ourselves. We had such a peaceful and relaxing break. What I realized over the break was that I had needed a break from Chan more than I needed a break from school. Keep in mind that I had presentations and midterms before the break. With Chan out of the picture, our apartment felt like a retirement home. Alex and I would get up in the morning and go on a walk to get breakfast. Then we would enjoy an afternoon activity like swimming or shooting hoops. Most of the time, we would end up doing both. Our nest wasn't completely empty, though. Drew was frequently over to partake in our apartment's amenities.

Our complex had a rectangular lap pool and a bean-shaped fun pool. The bean-shaped pool was fun because, for some odd reason, it was rarely occupied, while the lap pool was usually filled with small children. I think parents think the lap pool is safer because it isn't as deep as the bean pool. The lap pool is three to four feet deep while the bean pool has a depth of three to six feet. Can't a child drown in a foot of water? I don't see the difference in pool preference; if both pools are over a foot, a child can drown in either pool? I'm sorry this took a weird, dark turn. I didn't mean to get into children drowning, I just found it odd that parents, for the most part, only let their kids swim in the lap pool. This was unfortunate for any person wanting to use the lap pool.

The spring break pool experience was made even greater because Chan was not there. As you know, Chan does not like to follow pool rules, regardless of their hygienic importance. In the pool, Alex, Drew, and I would play a game called BTC (Ball Toss Catch). This is a game where someone tosses a ball. Another person catches the ball. Then it repeats itself. It may seem complex at first, but after a couple of tries, you get the hang of it. After pool time, we would eat dinner, have a drink, and watch some TV. This carefree, tranquil living went on for a week until Chan returned.

On the last day of break, Chan returned from San Diego. Alex, Drew, and I were eating ice cream and watching a half-naked guy running from the police on an episode of *Cops,* when the door was flung open. It was a tan Chan. He clearly had caught some rays. That's when we were hit with the sad realization that Chan was back.

This is how I would describe the feeling: Imagine walking through a park on a warm evening. It's the golden hour and the sun's golden rays creep through the treetops. You have your headphones in and you are listening to a happy, upbeat song. The air is filled with the aroma of flowers and freshly cut grass. It's warm, but you don't mind because there is a nice evening breeze. All of a sudden, you feel your foot have a little resistance as you step down. You stumble forward, jerk your head down to see what you stepped on. As you jerk your head, three sensory things happen. Your headphone falls out of your ear. You are immediately hit with the sounds of life—cars honking, dogs barking, birds chirping, and two girls loudly discussing last night's episode of *Vanderpump Rules*. The smell of flowers and freshly cut grass fades. An uninvited, foul smell begins to fill the air. As you look down at the bottom of your shoe, you see a steamy shit. When you see it, the smell intensifies. It's one of those pungent smells that you can somehow taste...

Basically, Chan returning felt like stepping in dog shit. Life was bliss before a tan Chan stepped through the door, just like the moment before you step in dog shit.

As we said our hellos, Chan quickly stripped down to his underwear, kicked his clothes into a ball, and rolled them up against the wall like a dung beetle rolls a shit.

"How was San Diego?" I asked.

"Amazing," said Chan. "We (referring to his computer/IRL friends) went to a club and the beach. We spent most of the time at the beach. It was real nice."

"Oh, that would explain the tan," said Alex.

"Yeah, my shoulders are all burnt. A good thing did happen, though. I met a girl."

"Ooooh," crooned Alex and I, harmonizing in unison.

"Yeah, she is from here, too."

"San Jose?" asked Alex

"Mhmm." Chan nodded.

"Really?" I asked.

"Yeah, I'ma try to hang out with her."

"You like her?" asked Alex.

"Sorta. I'm not sure what I want. I just asked her to be my friend and hang out."

We all looked at Chan.

"Did you use the F-word?"

Chan paused for a second. "Friend?" he asked.

I nodded my head and said, "Oh geez."

"You're screwed," said Alex.

"Goddammit, Chan," said a somber Drew. Chan's face looked unsure of what we were alluding to. Alex quickly pounced on the opportunity to clarify.

"Using that word is a one-way ticket to the friendzone."

I know all too well about that place.

"I want to be in the friendzone!" responded Chan.

"You friendzone yourself?" asked Drew.

"Yeah," said Chan. Chan doesn't seem to realize that there is almost no coming back from the friendzone. I like to think of the friendzone as the pit from *The Dark Knight Rises*; very few people escape (unless you are Batman).

"We have plans to hang out next week," said Chan, who I think had just realized that the friendzone may not be the safe haven he had thought it was.

"Well," I said, "good luck!" As I turned back toward the TV to resume watching a shirtless dude in jean shorts get tased, Alex caught my eye. He was staring at Chan. He was focused. He looked like a hawk spotting a field mouse.

Alex, with a confused look, asked, "What the fuck is that?"

"What? Where?" roared Chan.

"Right there," said Alex, pointing toward Chan's love handle. We all looked in the direction Alex had pointed.

"Dude!" exclaimed Drew. "Is that a booger?" On Chan's love handle was a little brownish-green ball, about the size of a jellybean.

"Maybe," said Chan, looking down at the booger ball.

Drew let out a stoner laugh: "UGHUH UH hUH hUH!"

Chan picked the booger off his love handle and flicked it into the trash. There was a brief moment of silence while everyone processed seeing a man casually pick a booger off his body. During this silence, I wondered how the booger had gotten there. *Did he pick it and rub it on himself? Did he pick his nose and flick it away with poor accuracy? Or perhaps he sneezed and propelled the booger onto himself? Yeah, that's probably it. I hope that's it.* The other options were gross, but then again, so was Chan.

"Where did you stay?" I asked, breaking the thought-provoking silence. "Hotel? Airbnb?"

"No. I stayed at my friend's apartment," he answered.

"How was that?"

"Alright. My friend's roommates got mad at me, though."

"What did you do?" I asked.

"I kept waking them up. My friend and I got super high and binge-watched *Family Guy*, which made me laugh."

"Oh, they thought you were loud?" I strategically asked, hoping to get Chan to self-evaluate.

"Yeah," said Chan.

Yes! I thought. *He said it, not me. Maybe this talk would give Chan some self-awareness. Ah, who am I kidding? A minute ago, this guy didn't realize there was a giant booger stuck to his body.*

"Sounds like you had fun," I said, hoping to end the conversation so I could return to watching TV.

"I'm tired from traveling, so I'ma go to sleep," said Chan, yawning.

A few days after the night of the mysterious booger incident, I was at my senior sem class and my professor had us stand in a circle and share something we did over break. A lot of people said they went to the Santa Cruz Beach Boardwalk. Santa Cruz is only about a forty-five-minute drive from school and it's got a great beach. When it was my turn, I just said I watched a bunch of Netflix. It's not the coolest or the most exciting spring break, but I'm comfortably basic.

After class, my professor wanted to talk and discuss my senior thesis project. Before we were released for spring break, the professor had assigned us homework. The assignment was to brainstorm ideas over the break for our senior thesis project. The structure of the project was broken down into two parts. The first part was a creative element and the second part was a written portion (at least sixteen typed pages). I told her I wanted to do a presentation on how dyslexic students struggling in school may benefit from alternative teaching methods. I informed her that I had dyslexia and struggled through school, so I had first-hand experience of the matter. I told her that I was going to make a documentary for my creative portion of the assignment. This would allow me to share my journey with dyslexia and how I was able to overcome it and manage to make it to college. When I said I was watching Netflix all spring break, I should've clarified and mentioned I was primarily watching documentaries as research, hoping I could get some inspiration and refresh on good interview angles. I had taken film production and screenwriting classes before. I like to think I had some idea of what I was capable of doing.

That evening after dinner, Chan was informing us that his "lady friend" (I used quotes because there was no evidence of her existence) would be coming over Saturday. That was nice of Chan to give us a day-and-a-half notice. Usually, he didn't give us a heads-up about anything.

"What are you guys going to do?" I asked.

"I think we are going to go to the beach," said Chan.

"Santa Cruz?" I asked.

"Yeah," Chan answered.

"That sounds like fun."

"I hope so," said Chan.

"Oh, my guy is here," interrupted Drew.

"What guy?" asked Alex.

"Weed guy?"

"Yup," said Drew, who was struggling to put his shoes on. Drew would occasionally order weed and have it delivered to our apartment. Every time he did this, I got nervous. I didn't want neighbors to report us to management. Drew's weed delivery guy was a hefty fellow, with a thick, bushy beard and long hair. He looked kinda like one of the stars of *Duck Dynasty*. Fortunately, the weed guy never came into the apartment. He would pull up to our street in a red Pontiac Fiero (a car that was way too small for him), roll down his window, and he and Drew would transact business.

"Get the bong ready," said Drew, rushing out the door.

"Kay," said Chan with a grin. A few minutes later, Drew returned with a brown paper bag filled with weed. He was grinning ear to ear. He and Chan tore through the bag and spent the next hour trading bong hits. Meanwhile, Alex and I watched *Shark Tank* and constructed a shopping list for our trip to the grocery store. Chan and Drew returned from their bong sesh. Drew joined us on the couch, while Chan chose to lay belly-up on the floor, half naked in his tiny boxers. These were his favorite boxers. They were white, with pickles printed all over them. As he laid on his back, he watched some videos on his cell phone while his legs wiggled around. Yeah, I don't know. Honestly, I don't want to know. All I know is that it was probably the most unattractive thing I have ever seen.

"Is there any cookie dough?" asked a high Drew.

"No, but we can add it to the list. Alex and I are about to go to the grocery store," I said.

"Oh, let me get in on that!" said Drew.

"You want to go with us?" I asked

"Hell yeah, dude," said Drew.

"I want to go too!" interrupted Chan. "I don't want to be here by myself."

"Well, we are leaving, like, now, so you better hurry up and put some clothes on," said an unamused Alex.

As much as I wanted Chan to stay, him coming with us was better than leaving him home alone. Chan quickly grabbed a pair of shorts and a shirt from a pile of his clothes that was, unfortunately, located in the living room. It was his classic look, with a twist. Beige cargo shorts and a small T-shirt—that was inside out. Once we were snug in Alex's small Subaru, Chan quickly and loudly asked if he could play his music.

Alex obliged and Chan grabbed the auxiliary cord. He fumbled with his phone for a couple of seconds until he could plug in the cord. While Chan molested his phone with the plug, we figured out which grocery store to visit. There was a store eight minutes away, in the hood, which also happened to be few blocks away from a strip club—so now you have an idea of the sort of clientele that grocery store has to offer. Or, we could go to a store fifteen minutes away, located across the street from Santa Clara University. We decided to go to the grocery store that was further away. On the way to the store, Chan did what he always did when we let him play music. After every song, he would ask if we liked it.

We pulled into the parking lot and found a spot in the middle of the lot, underneath a streetlight. When I exited the car, a bright reflection of light hit me in the eye. I looked down, only to see Chan's pale, bare feet reflecting the luminescent moonlight in my face. Chan was not wearing shoes. He didn't seem to notice that he wasn't wearing any shoes. As we approached the entrance to the store, all I could focus on was Chan casually strolling through the parking lot like nothing was afoot (especially shoes). You know how some business establishments post signs on the door that read, "No shoes, no shirt, no service"? I had always wondered who was walking into these places without shoes or a shirt. I finally had my answer. Thank God he had at least remembered to put his shirt on. I guess he hadn't even done that right—his small shirt was still on inside out.

This grocery store, in particular, always had attractive women there. For some reason, on this night, there was a huge uptick in the gorgeous girl department. The store was across from Santa Clara University, so we were surrounded by girls in our age range. Most wearing lululemon leggings. I can only assume a yoga class had just let out. After processing this intel, Alex and I quickly tried to distance ourselves from Chan so we wouldn't be seen as associated with him. We

Spilled Curry

strategically fell back behind Chan and Drew and let them lead. We made our way to the back of the store, where their perishable food was. Drew wanted to grab some milk to accompany the cookies. I took this opportunity to grab some half-and-half for my morning cup of coffee. At this point, our formation had reconfigured. Chan had slowed up and he was behind everyone, while Alex and I were in front, leading the group. Now that Drew had his cookie dough and milk, we headed for the checkout.

In front of us was a puddle of water, near the aisle where we had grabbed the milk. One of the refrigeration units sprung a leak, so we all stepped to the side of the puddle and continued toward checking out when we heard:

"Aw, geez!"

We all turned our heads to find Chan, standing barefoot in the middle of the puddle. The puddle of water quickly got diluted by Chan's filthy feet. Chan, in his altered state, began to freak out.

"Guys, what do I do?" questioned Chan in the loudest whisper I have ever heard. "What do I do?" he repeated, still standing in the puddle. "Get paper towels!" he whined in an outside-yet-still-inside voice.

After fighting the urge to laugh, I couldn't hold it in any longer. I burst out with laughter, which set Alex and Drew off. We all began to lose it. Just then, a group of gorgeous girls walked down this high-traffic aisle. I assume they were all models. I can only imagine how it looked to these girls.

Just imagine going to get milk and you have a six-foot-five, 300lb Chan standing barefoot in a dirty puddle, wearing a tiny, inside-out shirt. The girls didn't notice that Chan was in a puddle at first. It was only when they got close to him that they realized what was going on. They stopped in front of him and did what any normal people would do: collectively stare in awe. As I was trying to contain my laughter, I could see the girls trying to process what was happening. I don't blame them for staring. It was a lot to take in. Unfortunately for the model squad, this gave Chan a chance to turn to them and shout-whisper, "Do you have any paper towels? Or napkins?"

I began to tear up with laughter, but I was also a little embarrassed, so I quickly ducked into a nearby aisle, where I could still see Chan. Alex quickly followed me and took cover behind some baked goods. He, too, was a little embarrassed about being associated with Chan. Drew, on the other hand, didn't seem fazed by what was going on. He continued shopping and went to grab some beer. Alex and I just kept laughing at Chan, who was asking every passing girl in the store for paper towels. All while standing in a now dark, murky puddle.

Once the coast was clear, Alex and I went to retrieve Chan.

"Time to go," said Alex.

"I can't. I need napkins or paper towels; my feet are all wet."

"Your feet are all wet cause you are standing in a damn puddle," barked Alex.

"Well, I didn't know what to do," Chan answered.

At this point, Alex was annoyed. "Try stepping out of the fucking puddle," bellowed Alex. *Alex is going to make a great father one day*, I thought.

"Fine," groaned Chan. As we walked toward the checkout line, I began to laugh again because I noticed Chan was leaving size-fifteen footprints all the way to the checkout line. This was the last time we went to the grocery store with Chan. You would think that this would be the last time we went out in *public* with Chan. Unfortunately, it wasn't, and Chan's behavior only got worse, and twice as embarrassing.

The next day, I spent most of my time ordering books for my senior sem paper. Later that afternoon, I went down to the kitchen to heat up some dinosaur-shaped chicken nuggets. For all the numerous things in this world that taste like chicken, you would think some dino nuggets would be among them. When I made it to my room, I realized I had forgotten to grab a napkin. I put my bowl of dino nugs on my desk and headed back downstairs. As I exited my room, and entered Chan's loft, he slowly rotated his computer chair so that he was facing me. You know, the way they do it in the movies. Once facing me, he said, "Looks good, doesn't it?"

Chan purposely asked this vague question to bait me into asking him what looks good. After I reluctantly gave in, Chan said, "My room. I cleaned it. Feels so good to clean my room."

I glanced around the room and thought, *It literally looks the same as before. In fact, I didn't notice a difference when I walked through the first time with my nuggets.*

"Looks good," I said, lying.

"That girl I met in San Diego is coming over today!" bragged Chan.

"Oh, cool, are you guys still going to go to the beach?" I asked.

"I think so," he said.

"Well, I'm going to shoot hoops and go to the gym later, so have fun, man," I said.

After consuming my disappointing dino nugs, I texted Alex to come to my room. We often text each other to communicate in the household without Chan knowing. Once Alex was in my room, I whispered, "You see Chan's room?"

"Obviously," he said.

"I know you saw it, but he said he cleaned it, and it looks exactly the same to me."

Alex smiled. "Still looked dirty as shit to me."

Just then, we heard the shower turn on. I opened my door; Chan was downstairs, in the shower. We took this opportunity to scan Chan's room for any evidence of him having cleaned it. We just stood in the middle of his loft and looked around like we were at an open house.

"I guess he kinda cleaned it," I said. He had collected all the crap on his floor and piled it into a corner, and then stuck the rest of his junk into his cupboard. I know this because his cupboard door was broken and hung at a diagonal angle, allowing one to see the contents within. He had also piled his clothes to one side of his hamper. By hamper, I mean love seat.

Chan had a love seat in his room that served as a hamper. He used it to hold his laundry. Chan had taken the clothes that had been scattered all over it and pushed the pile over to one side. This would enable some lucky lady to have a seat and enjoy the company of Chan and his laundry pile. If this was his room clean, I would hate to see it when it was *dirty*.

"Looks like he missed a spot," I said, pointing to a dirt circle on the wall next to Chan's desk. It looked like something the soggy girl from *The Ring* would crawl through. Chan had a habit of resting his feet on the wall, which resulted in a massive dirt circle with a three-foot radius.

"Geez, his walls are dirty," said Alex. The wall next to Chan's bed had dirt streaks bordering it.

"He did throw out the cranberry juice container," I said.

"Ah, true," said Alex. A few months before this, when Chan had kidney stones, he drank a lot of cranberry juice. For months, he had subleased the crevice in between his bed and dirty wall to an empty bottle of Ocean Spray. I had begun to think that he would never throw it away.

We heard the shower turn off.

"Hoops?" suggested Alex.

"Yeah, let's do it."

We left to go play basketball. The situation in Chan's loft was rapidly turning into a bad episode of *Room Raiders*. Thank God we didn't have a black light.

That afternoon, we returned from basketball and neither Chan nor his lady friend could be found. I guessed they were still at the beach. Later that evening, Chan returned home in classical Chan fashion, by aggressively opening the front door. Alex ambushed Chan as a dog does its owner when it's been left home alone all day. Alex began to bombard Chan with questions, like "How was it? Where'd you go? What did you do?"

"It was good," said Chan, answering Alex's first question. I couldn't let Alex have all the fun, so I got in a couple questions as well.

"How was the beach?" I asked.

"Uh, we didn't go to the beach."

"Oh, I thought—"

"We went to the mall instead," interrupted Chan.

"Oh," I said.

"So, you and she do anything?" asked Alex, trying to provoke some locker-room talk, even though he knew nothing had happened. Chan wasn't very presidential, if ya know what I mean.

"Nothing really, we just walked around the mall for a bit."

"You show her your room?" I asked with genuine curiosity.

"Yeah, when she first got here."

"Why didn't you go to the beach?" I asked, scratching the stubble on my chin.

"She decided that she didn't want to do that," Chan told us.

"Not going to lie, but it seems to me like you're still in the friendzone," Alex said.

"Yeah, I don't know," said Chan.

I mean, Alex and I go walk around the mall all the time.

"I don't know what we are. I'm gonna take a break from girls," said a defeated Chan.

"Well, look at the bright side: at least your room is clean," I said.

Chapter 21 - Crashing

It was a few weeks away from my senior sem final presentations. I was standing in the hallway, waiting for the students of the class before mine to be let out so I could grab a seat for my class. As I was nodding my head to Kid Cudi's "Pursuit of Happiness," I felt someone tapping my shoulder. I turned to find Kimberley standing beside me. She had a tan glow and had her hair up. She looked gorgeous. Kimberley always showed up to class in two types of outfits: She either was dressed like she was going out to a dinner or dressed like she just got back from a yoga class. On this day, she was in a tank top and black workout pants with a racing stripe.

"Hey," she said, smiling. "How's your project going? The one for senior sem."

"It's good. I just finished an outline for all the shots for my documentary." *Whatever you do, Nick, don't look at her mouth, that's just weird. Just make eye contact. Wow! Her eyes are blue.* I began to get lost in her eyes.

"And I need fi—fi..." I was so lost in her Cookie Monster-blue eyes that I began to fumble my words. "Fa-ive, five! more pages for the rough draft that's due tomorrow."

"Oh yeah, I haven't started the paper part yet," she chuckled, peering into my eyes.

I felt like surveying the other students in the hallway: *Do you guys see this? You see this happening? You see this gorgeous girl making heavy eye contact with me, right? This is a moment, right?* I'm always dissecting and examining experiences in real time. Speaking of moments, I never had one moment of just being smooth with Kimberley, or any girl, for that matter. You can call me Not-So-Slick Nick. After class, I was sitting at my desk, and Kimberley walked by and gave me a wave.

"Good luck!" I said, giving her an upward head nod. I was very cool.

"For what?" asked Kimberley.

"On the paper," I reminded.

"Oh, yeah! Right. There goes my day, haha. Well, I'll see you tomorrow."

"See ya," I said.

When I got back to the apartment, I noticed Chan's front bike tire was smashed. It looked like Chris Christie had stepped on the rim of the bike. I parked my bike against the wall adjacent to the one where Chan had leaned his bike. As I was examining the tire, Drew returned from class.

"Hey, Drew, how's it going?" I asked.

"Oh shit!" exclaimed Drew. "What the fuck happened to that tire?"

"I don't know, I just got here," I responded.

"He crashed it," said Alex, appearing from his room. This conversation caused Chan to join us.

"Chan, you really crashed?" I asked.

"Uh, yeah," said Chan, descending the stairs in his boxers. *Could this day get any better? I had a great convo with Kimberley, and I come home to the joyous surprise of Chan crashing his bike?* I know I sound like a bit of jerk right now, but in my mind, this was karma. The week prior, Chan thought it would be funny to play a joke on us—by telling us he got in a car crash.

Of course, Alex and I believed him. No, not because he is Asian. Why would you think that would be the reason? No, he happens to be a bad driver who is Asian. I never knew what the gripped handles that hang above the windows of cars were for until I got in a car with Chan. Whenever Chan would drive down the ramp to exit our apartment complex's garage, he would ignore the stop sign located at the bottom of the ramp, where the driveway meets the sidewalk. He'd roll through to the street, which is incredibly dangerous. Someone walking their dog, or someone pushing a stroller, or someone on a bike could have easily been nailed by Chan. So, when he told us he got in a car crash, it wasn't out of the realm of possibility. In fact, it was highly probable.

"Are you okay, man?" asked Drew.

"Your bike's not," I said.

"I scraped my leg and my side," said Chan, turning his torso and showing off a tiny scrape.

"Well, that's what you get!" fired Alex.

"Huh? Why is that what I get?" asked Chan.

"Tell them where you fell," prodded Alex.

"I fell on the ramp."

"What ramp?" I asked.

"The one outside the business building," Chan explained.

I was very familiar with this ramp. It was a long, narrow ramp that bordered the outdoor yard area where the coffee shack was. I had seen Chan race down this narrow ramp blasting music from his phone (yes, he's one of *those* people), emitting a certain reckless negligence like he did when he drove down the driveway.

"So, you crashed into the ramp?" I asked, trying to piece together the event.

"Well—"

Before he could get the next word out, Alex interrupted. He clearly was excited and eager to share the juicy details.

"While he was riding down the ramp, there was a girl walking up it. So, to avoid a collision, he crashed into the rail."

"Really?" I said, trying not to laugh. *Dial it back, Nick.* Drew let out a sigh.

"Chan," said Drew, shaking his head.

"What? I didn't know she would be there," Chan said.

"You're an idiot for riding down a narrow-ass ramp where people walk," snapped Alex.

"It never happened before," argued Chan.

The location of the ramp was a high foot-traffic area. A lot of students hung out in that vicinity and enjoyed the coffee shack that was fifty feet away. I began to bite my lip to stop myself from laughing, because the image of Chan steering his bike into the rail to avoid hitting another student in front of tons of people was hilarious. Trying to pry more detail from Chan, I asked, "What happened? Were there a lot of people there?"

"Yeah."

"Well, did they help you?" I asked.

"No. Well, one guy asked if I was good."

The next day, Chan got up early (I know this because he started blasting music), played some video games, then left to go home to drop off his bike at his parents' house. He tasked them with getting it fixed. Since Chan was bikeless, this meant he would have to drive to school. Poor guy and his first-world problems. I, on the other hand, rode my bike to school feeling pretty good. I had completed the remaining five pages of my fifteen-page rough draft. While I was in the classroom eating, Kimberley walked in wearing matching yoga gear.

"Hey, you finish the draft?" she asked. While she awaited my answer, she took a sip of her frozen Starbucks drink.

"Yeah, I did."

"Get out! Really?" she asked in a surprised tone.

"Yeah, didn't you?" I asked.

"No, I still have like three pages to go, but I think it will be fine."

She began to frantically reorganize the desks in the classroom. "I hate desks," she said, as she was sliding them into a more orderly configuration.

"And yet you're a student?" I said.

She stopped shifting the desk and looked over at me. "Wh...why? What does that mean?" she asked in a sincere tone. Granted, my little joke wasn't very good. It was further tarnished due to the fact that I had to explain it.

"You said you don't like desks, and you encounter desks frequently when you are a student," I explained.

"Oh," she said, queuing an awkward but brief silence. "Can you watch my stuff? I gotta use the ladies' room," she asked.

"Of course," I answered. While I watched her stuff, some more of my fellow classmates trickled in, all wanting to know how much of the fifteen pages everyone had completed. One girl told me she had only written three, and another told me she had completed eight with pictures. *Wow, am I the only one who did the whole assignment?*

Kimberley returned.

"That bathroom is so gross!" she announced.

"Oh yeah?" I said. "I guarantee you, the men's bathroom looks worse."

"Probably," she said. "But the girl's room was pretty bad. I almost decided to hold it for this whole three-hour class!"

"Well, you're a survivor now; you seem like a stronger person, having endured such a trying experience," I said.

She gave me a half smile and began chatting with the other girls about the progress of their papers.

The professor was not pleased by the incomplete rough drafts. I wasn't worried. My paper was pretty much complete. I just had to get the filming and editing done, which would consume a majority of my time. At the end of the class, the professor was asking for volunteers to present on the first presentation day. As a class, we would be presenting for three class periods. I looked up from my desk and announced, "I'll go the last week, can we pencil me in for that?" I hoped that this would give me two extra weeks to work on my project.

The professor answered my request with, "Why don't you go the first?"

Great, now I have only a couple weeks to comb through my paper, buy props, film, and edit.

That weekend, I went home to visit and interview my mom and my sister for my film. I asked them to talk about my journey through school and how I had struggled with dyslexia. I also had my sister comment on tutoring methods that are most effective. She tutored for a private company that assisted with children who have learning disabilities. They gave great interviews, but I couldn't stay long because I had homework to complete.

Over the next couple weeks, I hit the books. I was grinding to finish school with good grades, like you're supposed to. Kimberley and I chatted before or after class, giving each other progress reports on our projects. I really enjoyed talking to her. I would offer some editing tips to her, because she was also making a video as her creative element to her project. Things were actually going great, for once. School was good, life was good, and my interactions with Kimberley were getting progressively less awkward (probably because I stopped staring at her mouth).

About a week before finals and presentations, I came home to find Chan's bike smashed, again. Only, this time, not only was the front rim smashed, his handlebars were smashed forward. Just then, Alex came in through the back door, carrying in some groceries.

"You see this?" I whispered, pointing to the broken bike.

"How?" mouthed Alex. We were being quiet because we were both unsure whether Chan was home or not. "Hey, Chan!" yelled Alex. No response. "Chan!" yelled Alex again. No response. I walked upstairs to put my stuff away, and also for reconnaissance to see if Chan was up there before we openly trash-talked him.

"He's not here," I said down into the living room at Alex.

I went downstairs to help Alex put groceries away. "So, what do you think happened?" I asked.

"I would not be surprised if he crashed on the same ramp again." We both were amused by the thought of Chan crashing twice in three weeks.

"He just got his bike back from the shop this week," I said, laughing.

Just then, Drew walked through the door with a bag of fast food, and a joint tucked behind his ear. Drew saw Chan's smashed bike and let out a noise that sounded like a combination of someone laughing and yawning at the same time.

"Yewhhhh, da fuck? Again? This shit just got fixed."

Drew inhaled his food and then began assessing the damage to the bike. We were all huddled around Chan's abused and battered bike, when we heard footsteps coming up the stairs to our apartment. I could tell it was Chan based on the vibrations he made when he walked up the stairs. Chan flung the door open to find the three of us looking at the abstract metal sculpture that had once been a bike.

Drew was on top of this. He quickly asked Chan about the bike. Clearly, Drew hadn't smoked yet. Chan reluctantly told us the story of how he crashed his bike, for the second time. Ahh, just when you think life can't get any better.

"Well, uh, I was riding back from class and I was next to this car, and it began to turn left. I guess he didn't see me, so I slammed my brakes, and I was leaning so far forward that my handlebars got pushed down and my tire-rim thing got bent."

I threw up both my arms and blurted out, "Hold up! You were on the left side of the car?"

"Yeah," replied Chan.

"Why?" I had to ask.

"I don't know, it's just where I ride," he answered

"Well, you're riding on the wrong side of the car," snarled Alex.

"There is a right side?" asked Chan.

"It's the RIGHT side!" I exclaimed. I want to say I was surprised at Chan's stupidity, but I honestly wasn't. He had crashed just weeks before. I had lived with this guy almost a year and had seen it all. I'd become numb to his moronic obliviousness. Chan is lucky to live in this time and age. Had he been alive years ago, he wouldn't have lasted very long. He would have been a casualty of natural selection. Then again, that may still be an option. He is the type of guy to try to pick a quarter off a train track during commute hours.

Chapter 22 - Finals Week

It was the most stressful time of the year—finals week. It's the time of year where you really buckle down. During this time, I was fueled by coffee, anxiety, and quick meals like canned soup and cereal. If I wanted to get fancy, I would make rice and sausages. I was like Mario Batali, without the ponytail and the sexual misconduct. I spent every day of finals week studying and preparing for my presentation. On this particular day, I spent all my time editing the film element of the presentation. I was due to present and premiere my film to my senior sem class in the evening. Editing took forever. I spent hours selecting the music. Thankfully, I was able to finish editing and arrive to class with just a few minutes to spare.

While the professor was hooking up the laptop to the projector, I began to give myself a pep talk. *Be confident, speak clearly, and look like I know what I'm talking about.* These qualities were in short supply. It didn't help that Kimberley was also in the class. The last time I gave a presentation in front of Kimberley, I got nervous and fumbled my words. This time, I had to stay focused. I wanted to get a good grade. I had put the work in; now I just needed to execute. I was due to present first. I surrendered to the confident persona to overcome my anxiety. A complete character recalibration. In order to accomplish this, I gave myself another pep talk. *You're going first, Nick. Sucks for everyone else. I'm about to set the bar real high. I'm what is referred to as a tough act to follow. Might as well give me an "A" now.*

I gave the class a brief intro on my thesis and process as to why I chose to make a film. Then, I let it play. I sat in the back of the class so I could be a creep and watch everyone watch my film. I had sprinkled some surprise jokes in the film, so I was trying to see if they landed, particularly with Ash and Kimberley. It felt good seeing a video I had created make Ash and Kimberley laugh. After receiving a ten-minute standing-O, I took questions from the class. Did I say ten minutes? I meant ten seconds. After I finished taking questions, everyone in the class filled out a comment form provided by the professor, which I would receive after class. This form was anonymous and would hold comments from my peers.

Now that I think about it, it wasn't a standing-O, it was a sitting-O, but I was standing at the time.

Now that my presentation had been completed, I felt a wave of relief consume me. I sat back and watched the three other students present.

The next person presenting was a girl named Sharon. I had no idea what Sharon's thesis was about. Her "creative element" was a ring that she had forged. The end of her presentation turned into a show-and-tell about a bunch of jewelry she had brought. The professor allowed us a few minutes to go up and inspect the jewelry, chat, and fill out the comment cards.

"These are cool," I said, looking at her ring collection. "You should open an Etsy store," I joked. Kimberley laughed.

The next presenter was Kimberley. Her thesis was about how music can be used as a therapeutic method to overcome depression. She talked about how certain music makes you feel different emotions. She also talked about how some people have synesthesia, which is the ability to see colors while listening to music. I'm curious if the people who claim to have synesthesia also take LSD when they listen to music. Kimberley's "creative component" was a video shot in a style to portray the sensation of being depressed. It was very artsy. During the Q and A portion of the presentation, I asked some Qs and gave her some compliments on her video. On the comment form, there were categories of the presentation that we were supposed to rate on a scale of one to ten, with ten being the highest. I gave her all tens. Then I added my own category, entitled "hair," to which I appropriately gave a ten. I thought writing that would be seen as cute or funny. Hopefully, both. I wasn't nervous about adding my own criteria, since the comment cards were anonymous.

The next scheduled presenter was Robbie. *Alright, here we go again.* Robbie's presentation was on the concept of creativity being a quality of a great leader, or something like that. His presentation had a very Wikipedia vibe to it. For his not-so-creative element, he had us grab our phones and open our web browsers. He directed us to a website that analyzed our personality types. It was similar to those Buzzfeed quizzes where you get to see which *Sex and the City* character you are, and yes, I'm a Carrie.

The professor was not very happy with Robbie. After his presentation, she said, "So, essentially, your creative component is an online quiz? Right? Unless I'm missing something?"

His face turned pale. "Yeah, but it's connected with my paper and my subject matter."

"Did you make the quiz yourself?" she asked.

"Well, uh, no. But I feel like it was tailored to my paper?" he answered. It was very awkward and yet thrilling to sit there while the professor dissected the whole presentation. While Robbie was being publicly executed, I sat back, knowing that I had nailed my presentation and had nothing to worry about. The only things that could have made the moment better would have been a margarita and some popcorn.

I know Schadenfreude is unfortunately frowned upon, but I can't help it if I occasionally have the feeling. Robbie was one of those "cool guys" who rarely showed up to class. When he did, he was fashionably late. I enjoyed seeing Robbie sweat, so much that I started smiling. I quickly had to cover my mouth and pretend like I'd caught a yawn. After the interrogation session, the professor seemed to realize the level of awkwardness this conversation had had on everyone who was not involved.

"Let's talk after class," said the professor.

"Uh, okay," said a flustered Robbie. I'm well aware that in this particular moment I seem like a jerk, but I was jealous. Life is tough when you're not the cool guy. People see Robbie and think he probably plays guitar and drives a motorcycle at the same time. People see me and think, *He probably has good credit*. Also, earlier this week, I had found out that Kimberley had been to Robbie's house to drop off some homework assignments while he was sick. This sucked, considering Robbie's relationship with Kimberley was far more developed than mine. Although, Robbie being sick would explain his absences.

Back at the apartment, I was heating up leftovers when I noticed an unopened envelope with a "La Playa" letterhead on the counter. I picked it up and walked over to Alex, who was sitting on the couch.

"You see this?" I asked.

"Uh, no, what's that? Chan forgot to pay rent again?" asked Alex, looking up from his laptop.

"No, I paid it," responded Chan from his loft. "I found that taped to the door earlier."

"You didn't bother to tell us?" questioned Alex.

"I forgot," groaned Chan.

"Let's see what this is," I said as I ripped open the envelope. The notice was just a routine letter notifying us that our lease was up in two months. If we planned to stay past the lease termination date, then the monthly rate would increase a couple hundred dollars. We had no intention of staying past our lease termination date. We were done with school in a week, and then we would have the apartment for another two months.

Later that evening, we were discussing if we could and should opt out of the lease and move out earlier. Alex and Chan seemed keen on it, so I said I'd have my mom, who is an attorney, check out the lease agreement and see if it was possible. They both agreed that was best. After our brief house meeting, we went back to studying for the rest of our finals.

The next week, I was in my last class, sitting at my desk and thinking to myself, *Fuck—Fuck—Fuck—Fuck—F-U-C-K!* I was having a minor anxiety attack while taking my last final. In the middle of my exam, it had dawned on me that this was my last final of my life, after being in school for over twenty years! *I'm finally in the position to be done. It took so much work to get here. I never thought I would be in this position—I wasn't supposed to be in this situation.* I had struggled for so long with my dyslexia. I thought about the beginning of my school career and how I had been labeled as having "behavioral issues" before I was tested for dyslexia. On my report cards, it had often said, "Can be a distraction to other students." I remembered the school wanting to hold me back in the fifth grade. I was reminiscing about the journey to get to this last final.

My mother, being an attorney, was able to convince the school to allow me to go on to middle school. It was in middle school where learned that students cheat. This was new to me. Cheating had never even seemed like an option. Knowing the guilt would overwhelm me, I never bothered with it. It's not my style. However, this didn't stop any of my fellow students. My literature arts class had a cheating ring. Every lunch before class, everyone would sit in the cafeteria and copy answers out of a workbook provided by two students who actually did the work. They eventually all got caught. After the teacher finished yelling at the class, I felt that it was unfair that I had been included in the yelling.

"I didn't cheat," I said.

"You're right," she responded. "You just didn't do it at all."

Welp, she had me there. I couldn't do it after school because that was skateboard time. Plus, I had a beef with homework. I mean, I spent eight hours at school. Then, because of my dyslexia, I had to spend hours after school struggling with homework, leaving very little free time. I couldn't do the homework at school. I was far too busy during lunch to do it.

During lunch, I would walk around school collecting money in a shoe box for my Air Force One fund. You see, at the time, the rapper Nelly was very popular. He had a song called "Air Force Ones." This made me not only want a pair, it made me need a pair. After two weeks of collecting students' leftover lunch money, one of the staff on yard duty walked over and asked what I was doing. I told her I was collecting money for my Air Force One fund.

"What are Air Force Ones?" she asked.

"Shoes," I said.

"I'm not sure if we can have you do that. Let's just run it by the principal." She was one of the nicer people on yard duty. That, however, was the last day I was allowed to collect money for Air Force Ones.

As I sat at my desk, I smiled and shook my head at this memory. This must have made my parents look so bad, having their kid collecting money from other students for shoes.

After middle school, I went to a strict Catholic school with the hopes of it shaping me into a disciplined young man. My mom had been promised there would be better resources for students with learning disabilities. It didn't, and there weren't. The only thing I got from that school was a case of Holden Caulfield Syndrome. It just felt like all the students and faculty were fake and phony. I didn't have very many friends. I would hang out with this kid who would, on occasion, take out his glass eye, my neighbor who went to the school, and the stoners. I never partook with the stoners; I just felt like they were transparent with their interest.

Most of my memories of that school aren't that great. I remembered being yelled at in front of my pre-algebra class for no reason. In that same pre-algebra class, I was daydreaming about basketball. Suddenly, without self-control, I made the motion of shooting a basketball. Everyone witnessed my shot, because I was seated in the front of the classroom.

"You make it, Nick?" shouted another student. I was mortified. I hated that class. Math has always been my nemesis. I needed to pass that and a few more math classes to graduate. Knowing that brought on a lot of anxiety that weighed on me.

I did have some good memories from Catholic school. There was a school pick-up football game that the juniors arranged. They planned that four teams would play, the freshmen, the sophomores, the juniors, and the seniors. This did not happen. I was the only freshman who attended. We just played a game with two teams and mixed the class types. I played pretty well. I have always been pretty athletic. I'm quick and I have always had a high vertical leap. These athletic abilities help me play well. So much so that, the next day, a senior jock-bro fella with diamond-stud earrings came up to me at lunch and asked, "Hey, man. Nick, right?"

"Yeah."

"Do you want to go to a party?"

Woah...I was overwhelmed. I had never been to a high school party. Out of fear of not knowing how to act at a party, I responded with, "No, that's alright."

"Really?" asked the jock-bro.

"Yeah. I'm good," I assured him.

"Well, it's a barbecue and there will be drinks. Let me know if you change your mind."

As I sat in my college classroom, the memories of transferring from that private school to a charter school began to fill my head.

The charter school was the complete opposite of the private school. The school itself was basically a giant room filled with students from sixth to twelfth grade. This school also had three portables where they would hold classes. This school was like Hogwarts for weird kids. At this school, there was this guy who would use paper clips to scoop ear wax out of his ears. Then he'd stare at his haul. When he wasn't doing that, he would be chowing down on some locally sourced boogers. He was gross-weird. The school was mostly filled with normal-weird. A lot of the students had dyed hair. You know? To collectively stand out as individuals.

There was another guy who often wore a black trench coat, even though it would be seventy-five degrees outside. Like, dude, I agree, *The Matrix* is an awesome movie, but you're making *me* hot, wearing that thing.

At the end of the day, I guess it's just teenagers trying to create themselves while enduring high school. In high school, students look all sorts of ways and wear all sorts of things. I remember, at this school, there was a kid who would always wear the color orange and a jester hat. You also would see the usual attire, like students with baggy pants, tight pants, yoga pants, and those cargo pants that unzip into shorts. There was an overwhelming amount of those. When I first entered the school, I felt like I had walked on to the set of *Mad Max: Fury Road*. Just a giant daycare of weird kids running around, and a pale, shirtless dude huffing silver spray paint. To my surprise, I seemed to fit in right away. The other students easily accepted me, despite the fact that I was the new, quiet, shy guy. My first impression of the school was very off-putting. I felt the school was a joke and everybody was phony (I clearly still suffered from Holden Caulfield Syndrome). I became less cynical once I made a few friends.

After I had gained the trust of the natives, I learned that this strange school just got stranger. I was informed that the school portables had been vandalized the year before. I'm well aware that the school being vandalized is sort of the norm in high school, but this wasn't your typical, run-of-the-mill vandalism. This was some *weird shit*. Which brings us to the *heinous act* itself. This school didn't have a "tagger," or "sticker slapper." No, those acts of vandalism are too cool for this school. Our vandal was the mystery pooper. The natives referred to this individual as "The Poo Poo Bandit." Yeah, I know. Someone the year before had sneaked into one of the portables and smeared poop all over the walls. *Yeah, that checks out*, I thought. News of the The Poo Poo Bandit did not surprise me. It fell in line with the school's M.O.

When I wasn't hearing about the tales of The Poo Poo Bandit, I found myself trying to find ways to stay entertained. My school provided a lot of free periods. I had quite a bit, since I was a junior and didn't have very many classes left. The free periods were designed so students could do their homework during school. I spent my free periods shooting hoops or tossing a frisbee in the back of the school. I would also do things that were slightly mischievous. I used to write down on a piece of paper, "I have always had a crush on you. Love, your secret admirer." Then, I would fold that paper into a paper airplane and throw it at an unsuspecting victim.

I would also write down things on Post-its and stick them on the backs of other students without their knowledge. They were like less violent "kick me" signs. I would write things like, "Ask me about my dog," or "I kissed a girl, and I'm still not sure if I liked it." This soon escalated to me drawing cartoon images and sticking them on other students. After honing my craft, I pushed things further, and began sticking random supplies on the backs of other students.

I would tape things like sugar packets, pencils, erasers, and parmesan cheese packets from Domino's. I once pulled socks out of the lost-and-found and stuck them on the back of an annoying student. The thrill of the possibility of getting caught fueled me. Once again, I took my antics to the next level and began sticking Post-its and cartoon drawings onto the backs of the teaching staff. This would all take place during my free time. I had another method to keep myself entertained in class.

In class, I came up with "The Word Game." Before every physics class, I would generate a list of random words and print copies of the list for every student in the class. As students entered the class, I would discreetly hand them a list outside the door before they went in. The objective of The Word Game was to use every word on the list before the lunch bell would ring. This being a physics class allowed some flexibility for integrating the words into the class discussion. For example, let's say two of the random words on the list are "cat" and "pineapple." You could ask the physics teacher, "Let's say a cat and a pineapple are dropped off a building at the same exact time. Which hits the ground first?" Dumb question, but that sort of sacrifice is what it takes to win the word game. I found tremendous joy in creating a game for the whole class to play. I made the most of my situation at this weird little school. The Word Game was truly one of my fondest memories of high school.

After not being accepted into any universities, I bounced around a couple of community colleges. I remembered having a panic attack outside my ASL (American Sign Language) classroom door. I had been out of town the first week of class and had emailed my professor, informing her that I would miss the first two classes. She responded to me with instructions to withdraw. She felt I would miss too much of the class, even though I would only miss two classes. When I returned from my trip, I checked the online portal and saw that I was still enrolled. I went to class to see if I could stay enrolled. When I arrived at the classroom door, I began to panic. I was told to withdraw. Yet, I found myself outside the classroom. I was going mad, running scenarios in my head. What would the professor say? Would I be publicly shamed? My head was racing, and my heart was beating fast.

As my hand reached for the classroom door, I could see my hand shaking as I grasped the knob. My anxiety was taking a physical toll on me. My head was hot, and I felt a throbbing pain in the back of it. If TV static was a feeling, that's how my head felt. I quickly retreated my reach for the knob. I took a deep breath. *Keep it together. Just go in there, man.* I turned the knob to see a quiet classroom of students. There wasn't much talking going, as this was a sign language class. The professor seated at the front of the class looked over to me, and she gestured with her finger, directing me toward her. When I got to her I said, "I know you said not to come in, but I noticed—"

"Shh!" she hissed. She began to jot down on a notepad.

"I'm still enrolled, so I—"

"Shht!" she hissed.

Really? Again? Being shushed is quite annoying, but twice in one day? Extra annoying. Oh my God! What is this woman's problem? I get this is an immersion class, but this lady is taking this sign language thing too seriously. The professor handed me the notepad. It read, "You can stay." I quickly sat myself at an empty desk. Halfway through the class, I realized the reason the professor had communicated with me via notepad was because she was, in fact, deaf. After such a rough start, this class ended up being one of my most memorable in community college.

Eventually, I was able to transfer to San Jose State University.

This was the end of my journey as a student. I had made it through elementary school without being held back, I had gone to a strict Catholic high school and then to a chaotic circus of a high school, and I had gone to multiple community colleges, to now find myself on the precipice of being done. *This is crazy—I'm about to be done forever. Well, shit, not if I can't complete this test. I gotta focus now. C'mon, man, you only have, like, thirty minutes to get this shit done. Why did I spend so much time daydreaming? Focus up and finish this thing. Finish, so at the end of all this, you get a piece of paper that says you accomplished something, and of course, the burden of student loan debt.*

I managed to get my shit together and finish the exam. I had come too far to completely lose it at the end. As I was packing up my things for the last time, I felt bittersweet. I was relieved to be done with school, but school was all I knew. I also felt a little down knowing that this was the last time I would see Kimberley.

I had grown to like Kimberley; we'd become very friendly toward each other. We always talked before and after class. I was dreading saying goodbye. I was going to miss our interactions. I was scrambling to figure out what I was going to say to her in this last interaction. Should I say anything to her? I was rapidly going through scenarios in my head as I packed up my backpack for the last time. As I swung my bag over my shoulder, Kimberley walked by and gave me a small wave. She smiled and walked toward the door. No, is that it? Really? Life is never like the movies.

As she got to the doorway, though, she slowly turned around and looked at me.

She looked radiant. I swear, her face glowed and sparkled. It may just have been the light reflecting off some sweat. Like I noted earlier, it gets hot in San Jose. But at that moment, her face sparkled like Edward Cullen's in the sun. Everyone around us disappeared and time slowed down, *just like* in the movies. The only noise I could hear was my own heart beating. I can't remember what we talked about, or how long we talked for. My trance-like state was broken when we hit a fork in the road. I had somehow managed to walk through the campus, chatting with her, until we were faced by a literal fork in the road.

"Which way are you going?" asked Kim.

"Oh, I'm going that way," I said, pointing to the left.

"Oh, well, I'm over here," she said, pointing in a different direction. It was the end of the road.

"Well, I hope to have a class with you again next semester," she said.

"I do too," I lied. I knew full well that I was done with school. For her, this was "see ya later," but for me, this was "goodbye."

"Have a great summer," she said, smiling.

"Uh, yeah, you too. Have a good one," I said back to her.

I stood there and watched her fade away into the distance.

I was standing there, dissecting everything, trying to figure what I should have done or said, while the other students walked past me. I was analyzing all the moves I had made, or should have made. Another cool fact about me—as a child, I was a member of the chess club. So, I often revert to my training and try to think a couple of moves ahead. Unfortunately, life is unpredictable and, for the most part, not like the movies. I was overwhelmed with bittersweet emotion. I felt like this was the end of any shot I had with Kimberley. This felt like goodbye forever. I finally walked back to gather my bike and my thoughts. The bike ride home felt like the longest ride of my life. I kept replaying the scene in my head, running through the wouldas, couldas, and shouldas. I felt my heart sink into my stomach. *I could have been smoother. I wish I was smoother. Maybe I'm just not cool enough, tall enough, strong enough, smart enough, funny enough.*

Hold the phone! Even if I accepted all this self-doubt, the one thing I now had was a college degree. That was something I had thought I would never achieve. I had thought that from an early age. I remember, in elementary school, some kids I thought were my friends refused to work on a group project with me because, and I quote, "Nick is stupid." By earning a bachelor's degree at San Jose State, I had reached a pinnacle which I had previously believed was beyond my grasp. *I may not be the cool, smooth-talking, buff dude who gets the girl, but who gives a shit! It could be worse. At least I'm not Chan.*

Back home, I was able to decompress after a couple of glasses of wine. All I could think about was Kimberley. I hated how it had been goodbye forever with her.

Maybe it didn't have to be. Especially since I happen to live in a time where it is fairly easy connect with people through social media. I made an effort to extend an olive branch to Kimberley. I quickly tried to find her on Facebook and Instagram but had no such luck. *Hmm, she's probably one of those people who uses a screen name that is different from their real name. I guess it was never meant to be. Wait, I've got it!* I logged into our class website and searched for her. We had a class website that nobody really used, but it was worth a shot. It was a long shot, at that.

I was able to find her student profile and send her a message. Forty-five minutes and three drafts later, I sent, "It was great to have met you, let me know if you ever need anything, here's my social security number. (555) 555-5555." I was so nervous. My hands were sweaty, and my heart was racing. I couldn't believe I was this much of a hot mess just trying to message somebody. At least this way, there was now a bridge of

communication.

After the dust settled, Chan, Drew, Alex, and I made plans to celebrate school's end by bar-hopping downtown. This would prove to be the most regrettable public outing we ever had with Chan.

Chapter 23 - Night on the Town

Well, we did it. We survived college unscathed (minus Chan's two separate bike injuries; other than those, we did it). This meant celebrations were in order. We did some Googling and compiled a list of cool bars to visit. After that, we got ready to hit the town. Cue the *Jersey Shore*-like montage of everyone getting ready, just with less spray tan and hair gel. I wore jeans and a button-up and my leather jacket. Alex wore a hoodie and jeans. Drew wore a hat, jeans, a t-shirt with two holes in it, and a light jacket, which also had holes in it. Chan's garb threw us for a curveball. We had all assumed he would be in his usual Chan attire (cargo shorts and a tiny t-shirt). To everyone's surprise, he was in a blue dress shirt and blue jeans. Radiating from Chan was a visible cloud of cologne. He smelled like the makeup department at Macy's. Wow! Despite him smelling like a cab driver from the '70s, he was appropriately dressed. I thought we were starting to rub off on Chan.

I had been out with Alex and Drew before. I was curious to experience being out with Chan. The feeling was like being in possession of fireworks—either everything was going to work out and it would be an exciting night, or everything was going to go wrong and blow up.

"The Uber will be here in fifteen minutes," said Alex, looking up from his phone.

"Hey, let's kill this bottle," said Drew, holding a near-empty handle of rum.

"I'm down for a little pregame," said Alex.

"Yeah, let's do it," said Chan.

Drew began to pour everyone a shot, when Chan insisted on having a full glass of rum because he didn't want to spend money at the bars. I was caught off guard by Chan's request. I understood the method to Chan's madness, but he wasn't much of a drinker. I mean, he would occasionally have a beer, but hard alcohol? The guys just wanted to pregame. Chan was asking for a doubleheader. Plus, Chan probably would have a mild tolerance, since he rarely drank. On the other hand, he is a very large human being. Perhaps a shot to me equates to a full glass to him? Maybe the scales even out? I don't how science works; I'm a creative arts major, after all.

"Are you sure?" asked a hesitant Drew, responding to Chan.

"Yeah, I'm going to get buzzed here."

"You're going to get more than buzzed!" said Alex.

"It's fine," said Chan, snatching the bottle from Drew. Sure enough, he poured himself a full glass of rum. Why he would want to drink a glass of straight rum to save money was beyond me. What he was doing seemed like the consequence of losing a bet. I would pay money to not drink a glass of rum. But this is Chan we are talking about; he defies logical comprehension.

Chan began to inhale his glass of rum. It was disgusting and made me feel nauseous. Is second-hand alcohol poisoning a thing? Captain Morgan himself would not have wanted to drink this much rum. Chan was two-thirds of the way through his binge when Alex announced, "Uber is almost here. Let's wait outside."

We put our shoes on and headed for the door. Everyone but Chan had their shoes on. *Oh no! Here we go again...Is he really going to forget to put shoes on again?*

"You going to wear shoes or what?" asked Alex. Good, I wasn't the only one who had noticed.

"Yeah," said Chan. He brushed by his usual pair of shoes and pulled a plastic container out of the closet near the front door. This plastic container was filled with shoes that Chan rarely wore. My first thought was that he was, in fact, capable of storing shoes somewhere other than the living room floor.

Chan pulled out—I kid you not—purple and orange Nike basketball shoes.

"These are my fuckboy shoes," said Chan, proudly, as he pulled the shoes out of the container.

"You had those the whole time?" asked Alex.

"I wear them when I need to fuckboy around," said Chan, jokingly.

"No, I mean you could have worn those when we played basketball," suggested Alex.

"I guess. Are they basketball shoes?" asked Chan.

"I mean, it says 'hyperdunk' right there," I said, pointing at the large shoe. "It has dunk in the title," I added.

"Oh, yeah, I don't know," said Chan.

"You could have worn those and probably have not fallen over," said Alex.

"Yeah—*murburgh!*" burped Chan.

Chan slid the shoes halfway on his feet, with his heels sticking out of the shoes. He then began stomping around like he was putting out a small fire.

"Dude, stop that," ordered Alex, looking vexed, arms crossed.

"What?" asked Chan.

"You can't do that. We have neighbors below us."

"Oh, I forgot," said Chan. Chan was trying to do the trick little kids use when they're too lazy to put shoes on like any normal person. He was trying to stomp his foot into the shoes. This juvenile method would never work. Chans feet were too wide to stomp into the basketball shoe. Once we were outside, we watched Chan stomp around while we waited for our Uber.

"He's going to scuff those things up before he even gets them on," I said to Alex. After a few seconds, he gave up and sat down. Surprisingly *without* the aid of two shoe-horns and a tube of KY, he managed to get the shoes completely on. He was now presentable from the ankles up.

Our Uber driver arrived. Alex, Drew, and I quickly piled into the back three seats, leaving the seat next to our driver for Chan. As we were buckling up, Chan turned to our Uber driver and shouted, "THESE GUYS WANT TO GO TO THE HOTTEST GAY BAR IN TOWN!"

The packed car was quiet. The Uber driver did not respond, and I couldn't blame him. It seemed like the effects of the rum were kicking in.

"That's not how Uber works," I said, responding to Chan's embarrassing outburst.

"It's not?" As we began our route to our destination, I had to explain how Uber works to Chan.

About halfway toward our destination, Chan began to burp profusely. Chan was then struck with the brilliant idea of trying to blow his burps at us. Unfortunately for our driver, Chan didn't have much neck flexibility. He ended up blowing his burps toward our driver. He did his hilarious burp-and-blow routine all the way to the bar. I was surprised our driver had kept his cool the whole way there. He could have driven in the wrong lane and I still would have given him five stars for tolerating Chan. We couldn't have arrived at our destination any sooner. I was relieved the ride was over. We were all mortified at Chan's behavior and how we were associated with him.

After our driver sped off, Alex scolded Chan, "Dude, what the fuck is your problem? That was rude as hell."

"What? I was just blowing burps at you guys," he answered.

"You were blowing them at the driver," snapped Alex.

"Oh, I didn't know," said Chan.

That was Chan's excuse to most things.

"I didn't know," he moaned again. What did he know? Because it didn't seem like a lot.

Drew eased the mood by saying, "C'mon, guys, let's get some beers and play some bp. I hear they got a bunch of tables in the back."

We stayed at this western-themed bar for about an hour and then decided to hop to the next bar on our list. At this point, Chan was so irritating, I got sober just by proximity. For some reason, he would only speak in an outside voice. As we were walking to the next bar he proclaimed:

"I WANNA FIGHT SOMEBODY. I WANNA FIGHT SOMEBODY. I WANNA DANCE, TOO! I WANT TO FIGHT AND GO DANCING."

I'm all for exercise and cardio, but do that on your own time. Chan was such a hot mess that it took all three of us to keep him at bay. Now we knew what it was like to be a diaper. We were the only things keeping this piece of shit contained.

"I WANT TO GET IN A FIGHT TONIGHT! I THINK I WOULD WIN," announced Chan, punching and kicking the air.

"You're not fighting anyone tonight," I said. As we continued our walk to the next bar, Chan heard music from a club across the street.

"I WANT TO GO THERE," yelled Chan, pointing to the club.

"It's not on the list," I said.

"I WANT TO CHECK IT OUT REAL QUICK." Chan then took off across the street to peek at the club. Alex and I both just looked at Drew. Drew knew it was now his job to go round up Chan. After Chan's brief observation of the club, we continued to the next bar. We continued on parallel sides of the street: Alex and I on one side, Drew and Chan on the other. Chan was now Drew's problem.

We arrived at a jazz bar, where we were stopped by a douchey doorman in a V-neck and blazer.

"Hold up, guys, there's an optional cover," he said.

"What? There is an optional cover? So, there is not a cover?" inquired Alex.

"There is one, it is optional," replied the doorman, adjusting his quiff.

"So, do we have to pay to get in or not?" Alex asked.

"You don't, but if you like to give money for the live music, you can," responded the doorman. So, we walked in without paying the cover. At this point, Chan had gotten to be too much to handle, so we were in a mood and couldn't care less about the live music. They could have been playing from an iPod, for all I cared. Chan had, once again, ruined jazz for me. At this point, we were just there for the bathroom.

After everyone had done their business, we traveled to our final bar. We cut our list very short, since Chan was too much of a wildcard. This final bar we went to was a karaoke bar that Chan was especially psyched about. Chan went straight to the DJ table to sign up to sing. Alex and I went to grab drinks for everyone. Drew grabbed us a booth. #teamwork

During every Karaoke set, Chan found it necessary to heckle the other Karaoke singers. He would yell out, "YOU STINK! WHEN IS IT MY TURN TO SING? I WANT TO SING!" Yes, he is the kind of person to heckle karaoke singers. We were all mortified. Luckily, our booth was right next to the speaker, so I don't think anyone but us heard Chan rudely heckling karaoke singers.

"GET OFF THE STAGE! YOU SUCK! I WANT TO SING! JUST LET ME SING, DAMMIT!" Chan did this for about an hour, while I kind of sunk into the booth. Finally, it was Chan's turn. He jumped out of the booth and bulldozed his way through the crowd up to the DJ. He whispered into the DJ's ear. Chan then hopped on stage and grabbed the mic. Music began to play, and Chan began to gyrate and bounce around. He then began to shout-scream Michael Jackson's, "P.Y.T." (Pretty Young Thing). Honestly, he was amazing. I mean, he sounded like shit, but the pageantry and stage presence really sold the performance. He would bounce up and down in a lunge position, and then jump up and down. When he sang, "I WANT TO LOVE YOU," he would do a quick twirl and then pick up from where he left off. "PRETTY YOUNG THANG!" He was hitting all the right beats. He looked like he had done this performance before. In fact, his performance almost seemed rehearsed. It was like he had choreographed and practiced and then waited his whole life for the opportunity to perform it. It was magical and almost made up for the humiliating situations he put us in.

This was the happiest I had ever seen Chan. At the end of his performance, people gave him quite the applause. While getting off stage on to the dance floor, he received some high-fives from some cougars. I can relive this moment forever because Alex managed to get a lot of it on camera, despite the poor lighting of the room. I had a good time watching Chan on stage fooling around, primarily because he was away from me. Chan had a great time and ended up doing what he had wanted to do all night—dancing and getting in a fight with the right vocal pitch.

Chapter 24 - Summer

Well, it was officially summer, and my days enduring Chan were coming to an end. It turns out, my days were more numbered with Chan than I'd thought. A few days after our infamous night out with Chan, he delivered some amazing and yet confusing news. Alex and I were in the living room watching TV, and Chan was in the kitchen making food and a mess. It was at this moment when he said, "Hey, guys, I found a new place. So, my dad's coming over on the weekend to help me move my stuff out."

"Wait, you're moving out?" Alex asked.

"Yeah!" he answered.

"We still have two and a half months on the lease here!" said Alex.

"I know, but I thought we can opt out?" said Chan.

"Oh yeah, my mom read the lease," I responded. "She said that there is a penalty of one month's rent to opt out early and you have to give thirty days' notice. So, in order for that to work, we would pay this month and next month, and then move out one month early, and at that point, I would rather stay the duration of the lease," I explained.

"Same," said Alex. "That's what we signed up for anyway."

"Oh, okay," said Chan. He went to his room and ate his meal, and then took off to volunteer at a dog shelter. He had developed a new method to meet girls. Chan would volunteer to feed the homeless and assist at a dog shelter. Then he'd brag about it.

Once Chan was out of the apartment, Alex and I began to gossip like schoolgirls.

"I can't believe he's moving into a new place. I mean, I'm glad he's going to be outta here, but we still have two and a half months left on our lease. School doesn't start up again for four months," I said.

"He's an idiot," said Alex.

"Now, he's going to be paying rent for two places. I know it's good to get a place early, but this early? Why?"

Chan is an enigmatic paradox, so trying to comprehend Chan's actions is a waste of time. Plus, this was good news, after all. Now, we could be rid of Chan and enjoy our summer, all the while having him continue to pay rent (poor planning on his part). My sentence living with Chan had been lifted and it felt great. I felt like an inmate who got let out early for good behavior. Now, my summer vacation actually began to feel like a vacation.

Unfortunately, my summer was cut short. Like Chan's tenure with us. My counselor notified me that I was four units short of the graduation requirement. This meant I wasn't graduating, and that I now had to take summer school classes. Why me? Of course this would happen. Graduating on time would be too easy. Ugh, now I would have to spend my summer studying quantitative statistics. I was stuck taking this course because it was the last online four-unit class available. One last hurdle before graduating and accomplishing something I never thought possible. Scratch that, plausible. It wasn't all bad, though. It was summer, after all, and Chan was going to be gone.

That evening, Chan decided to make crepes. It was moments like these that made me think he wasn't so bad. But then, these thoughts would instantly dissipate. I would recall all the moronic, tumultuous situations Chan had imposed on us, thus canceling out the rare generous behavior he would display. Chan simply making crepes for us was apparently easier said than done. While we were in the living room watching Tarek and Christina El Moussa argue about which tile backsplash to go with on *Flip or Flop*, we heard him shriek, "AH! SHIT-DAMN!"

"Everything okay in there?" asked Alex, glancing over his shoulder into the kitchen.

"Um, I think so," said Chan, sucking his left index finger.

"Did you cut yourself?" questioned Alex.

"Yeah, I was trying to slice some bananas. I'll be alright," said Chan. "Can one of you get me a Band-Aid?"

"Sure," I said. I went under the kitchen sink and grabbed a first-aid kit. While I was fishing a Band-Aid out of the kit, Chan washed his wound in the sink and then wrapped it in a paper towel. Chan stepped into the dining area and over to our table, where I had opened up the first-aid kit. Once I got a Band-Aid out, I could see blood rapidly soaking through the paper towel.

"Hey, Chan, let's take care of this in the bathroom," I suggested.

"No, it's fine, I just need a Band-Aid." Just then, the blood started dripping off of Chan's finger and plummeting to the carpet.

Chan seemed to be unfazed by the fact that his finger now looked like a used tampon.

"Chan, let's take this into the bathroom, or at least the kitchen," I repeated.

"I'm great, here is fine."

"Dude, there is blood dripping onto the carpet, and that shit stains," I said.

"Oh," said Chan. He then took a couple steps back, retreating into the kitchen. Finally, I found an appropriately sized Band-Aid for Chan's large, bloody finger. In our kit, we had an overwhelming amount of the tiny, circular Band-Aids, but those would not be able to get the job done. As it turned out, no Band-Aid would get the job done. Once I was in the process of applying the Band-Aid, I made eye contact with the wound. It was a deep gash. I looked up at Chan and said, "I think you are going to have to get stitches."

"It'll be fine," said Chan. "It's just a cut."

"Cut? Dude! That's a flesh wound!" I said, trying to hint at the potential urgency of the situation. Alex ran over to investigate the scene. Apparently, the idea of Chan going to the hospital had piqued his interest.

"Dude, your Band-Aid is already soaked," said Alex. "I think Nick's right; you're gonna need stitches."

"It's alright, guys, really," said Chan, wrapping his finger in a paper towel for the second time.

"Look, if that doesn't stop bleeding, then you have to go to the hospital," I said in a paternal tone.

"I'm going to lay down for a bit," said Chan. After about ten minutes, we heard Chan on the phone with his parents in a real somber voice. The only thing I could make out from eavesdropping was Chan saying in a soft but worried tone, "I didn't know." This was always Chan's first, instinctual response to most things. He then peeked over the loft edge and said, "Hey, guys, my parents are coming to take me to the hospital."

"Good," snapped Alex.

"Better safe than sorry," I said.

"Get well soon, Chan Man," said Drew.

When Chan returned from his field trip to the hospital, he came back with two stitches and a roll of gauze so he could change his bandages daily. I can only imagine if he had been home alone when he had cut himself, he would probably have bled out.

A week later, Chan and his dad were over, moving his stuff out. This meant I spent my afternoon listening to Chan and his dad casually yell over each other. In an effort to expedite Chan out of my life, I offered to help them move. Chan, unfortunately, declined the offer. *Dammit, this asshole is going to take his sweet time.* So, I retreated to my room to re-watch an episode of *Chelsea Does*, when I discovered a text on my phone from Kimberley. That's right, a response, finally! I had been checking my computer for a response every day for the last week. I had reached the sad conclusion that she had never received my message or, more realistically, was not interested in talking with me. I was a little down. I'm somewhat of a hopeless romantic. Did I say hopeless? I meant helpless. I was delighted that I had received a response, even if it was weeks later.

In response to my message that read, "It was great to have met you, let me know if you ever need anything, here's my social security number. (555) 555-5555," she responded, "This appears to be your phone number. I need your SSN."

I replied, "My bad, I always mix the two numbers up. I have had my identity stolen an overwhelming amount of times. I'm assuming you'll want my credit card numbers too?"

"Yes, please send!" she replied. We jokingly texted back and forth, but the texts faded after a couple days and I haven't heard from her since. There were more pressing matters to deal with, like the mess Chan left.

While Chan was moving his junk out, I went to the mailbox, where I found a letter from the management office. *Great*, I thought, *what did we do now?* I walked back to the apartment and read the letter. To my relief, it was just a standard pre-moveout checklist regarding the condition of the apartment and how to acquire all or most of our deposit back from La Playa management. The letter recommended cleaning the apartment and patching any holes in the walls. I showed Alex and Chan the letter.

"We gotta clean the place up before we go, so we can get our deposit back," I said.

"We should just hire a cleaning service," suggested Chan, who was putting a duffle bag of clothes over his shoulder.

I nodded my head and agreed, "Yeah, that's a good idea."

Chan said goodbye and left.

"Freedom! He's gone! He is finally gone!" I exclaimed. Alex and I fist-bumped. It was a joyous feeling. It was such an overwhelming sense of relief, like when Dorothy threw a bucket of water on the wicked witch. #Byebitch

"Hey, let's go in his room," said Alex.

We rushed up the stairs to see Chan's empty room and to feel some closure.

"What the fuck did they do all day?" said Alex, staring into Chan's filthy loft, still occupied by his junk. Had they just moved his clothes and bed out and called it a day? There was an overwhelming amount of dirt smudges, and blood from Chan's leaky finger, on the walls bordering his bed. It looked like a shitty cave painting. I felt like I was a CSI and our suspect was sloppy. He had left fingerprints, hair samples, blood, and probably semen at the scene of the crime. Chan had also left his desk and a stack of dirty dishes. *Geez, no wonder he wanted to hire a cleaning crew; that's what it would take to get this room cleaned.* I walked into the closet that Chan and I shared. He had taken about half his clothes and left a couple suitcases.

Chan was just the worst. He is repugnant and repulsive; it was no surprise that his room did not reflect anything else. I'd had my high hopes, but it was too good to be true. I took his junk-filled room as a personal attack on my senses. His room was an eyesore that smelled awful. There was a hot, thick, musky air that lingered in his room. Alex and I launched a counter assault against Chan's lingering scent by crop-dusting Chan's room with Febreze. We then aired out the room with a couple of fans. Alex texted Chan about the stuff he had left behind. Chan said he would return in a couple weeks to get the rest of his stuff.

Life was bliss for the couple of weeks that Chan was gone. There were no injuries, no fires, and no Trump speeches. I spent most of my time on my online course, studying the material for my quantitative statistics class. This class, as you can imagine, is heavily math based. I'm a creative arts major; I have spent a majority of my college career avoiding math, which is why I chose the major I did. Being dyslexic, math has never been my strong suit. Math to me is like oil to water; it never really sinks in. So, in a cinematic fashion, it seemed only right for me to reunite with my arch-nemesis, math, as my final obstacle to graduation. What I'm trying to say is that math was my final boss in college.

Over summer, I would take breaks from studying to go swimming or to the gym. One Friday afternoon, Alex's brother Cody came over to hang out and enjoy the pool with us. Cody was a senior in high school and would be attending SJSU that upcoming fall. During Cody's visit was when I was introduced to a game called "Pokémon Go." Cody begged me to download it and play with him. I must admit, it was a fun, new, addicting game. You walk around town and catch creatures that don't exist. It was all the rage that summer.

While hunting for some Pokémon, Alex and I got a text from Chan, informing us that he was coming over to get the rest of his stuff to move into his new apartment. Alex and Chan texted back and forth. Alex, surprisingly and kindly, invited Chan to come over the next day to hang out and barbeque with us. Alex can be nice and friendly sometimes. This metamorphosis of demeanor usually happens after a couple of beers, which is what it took for Cody and me to get Alex to go out and catch Pokémon with us. It was like a reverse Jekyll-and-Hyde situation. He drinks and gets nicer. Alex was in such a good mood, he bought the meat to cook for everyone. Apparently, a couple of weeks without Chan can do wonders for the soul.

The next day, Chan came over in the afternoon. Chan, being the diva he is, had to make an entrance, so he did his classic bit where he flings the door open at a hundred miles per hour. I feel like he missed his calling to be the guy on a SWAT team who breaks through a door during a bust. What a missed opportunity. Chan would be a natural. Chan walked in sporting his usual attire of cargo shorts and a small t-shirt. Chan began telling us how great his life was without us.

"My life is pretty set right now. I got my new place and I begin my job at Oracle soon. Since money and work won't be an issue, I want to get a dog and then get married in a couple years." Gross, he wants to marry a dog? I knew what he meant, but my interpretation seemed more plausible. Chan then proceeded to tell us about his amazing new roommates. Without being asked, he mentioned that his new place is located closer to the school. Chan then peppered in some useless tidbits, like that his new place had a ton of on-street parking. It also had a bigger kitchen. He really emphasized the kitchen being larger than ours. He continued to brag about how happy he was in his new place with his new kitchen.

"Let's swim!" I announced, cutting off Chan bragging about his new, larger kitchen. In Barney Stinson fashion, I suited up.

The pool was empty, which meant we had the place to ourselves. Like boys being boys, we spent a good amount of time being rowdy and throwing a ball back and forth. After an hour of jumping in and out the pool and playing some good ole BTC, we went to soak in the hot tub. Chan insisted on doing some laps to get a workout in. So, Drew, Cody, Alex, and I were relaxing in the hot tub when all tranquility was shattered by a loud, shrieking groan.

From the hot tub, I could see Chan holding his big, round head, which was poking out of the surface of the pool.

"Urhhhhhhhh! Urhhhhh!" moaned Chan. It sounded like two majestic whales mating. Chan began to frantically rub his forehead.

"You okay, man?" asked Drew from the hot tub.

"I SWAM INTO THE WALL!" roared Chan from the pool.

At the time, all I could think was how thankful I was that nobody was around to see this. Chan joined us and dipped his feet in the hot tub.

"You alright?" I asked.

"Yeah, it just hurt," he said.

"Can you see straight? You don't have a concussion or anything?" I questioned.

"I'm fine," murmured Chan.

After we barbecued, Chan wanted to go catch some Pokémon. We all went on a walk. On our walk, I kindly reminded him to make sure to pay me for the June utilities.

"Oh, alright," said Chan in a soft voice. I could tell he was reluctant, since he had most of his stuff out. He still had some of his stuff in the fridge and freezer. He also had his computer and monitor still hooked up in his room. After a while, we wanted to go back to the apartment. By we, I mean Cody, Alex, and I. Chan had a different idea. He wanted to walk to Japantown to catch more Pokémon. We were tired and went back to the apartment, leaving Chan to hunt by himself. I went to bed early that evening. I was exhausted from catching all the non-existent Pokémon.

The next morning, I went downstairs to get my first of many cups of coffee. I opened my room door, only to discover that Chan had still left things in the apartment. He had taken all of his clothes, his computer, and his monitor. But he'd left a giant luggage bag filled with stuff, and an old-person shopping cart, which he had parked in the living room and never used, amongst many other items. This meant that Chan, unfortunately, would have to return...Or would he?

Chapter 25 - Fuckin' Chan, Man!

Oh my God. This is it. I'm done. I'm really done, I thought, sitting in front of my computer. I had just submitted my portion of my group project for my quantitative stats class. I was officially done with school. *There better not be any more surprises about not having enough units,* I thought jokingly to myself. *I'm done. I gotta do something!* I went to the gym to decompress, think about my future, and figure out what I was going to do with my life. Obviously, I spent most of my time in the gym thinking, rather than lifting. That would explain the lack of gains. I took a break to check my phone, to see if there were any good Pokémon nearby (yes, I still played that game). I was excited to see that there was a Charmander—right next to me! *Holy smokes! Time to catch this little stinker.* What a great, momentous day for young Nicholas. I threw a Poké Ball at Charmander, and it escaped. I threw another Poké Ball at Charmander, and he escaped again. *Third time's the charm,* I thought. I threw my third Poké Ball at Charmander, and he escaped again and ran away, thus eliminating any chance for me to catch him.

"FUCK!" I yelled down at my phone. I saw something to my left and looked over to find a girl standing in the doorway to the gym.

You think she heard that? I thought. *Of course she did,* I answered myself. I quickly did a set of half-assed sit ups, pretending to be nonchalant about my inappropriate outburst, and quickly got out of there. Welp, that was embarrassing. I'd had a real reaction to a non-existent event. Yes, Charmander ran away from me, and I got mad. But, Charmander had never really been there in the first place. So, I had gotten mad at nothing. Fuck Charmander; I don't see what makes him so charming. *How dare he make me look like a fool?* He immediately became my least favorite Pokémon. Fortunately for Charmander and his friends, I stopped playing the game because there was too much work to be done at the apartment.

T'was the last week of living at La Playa. Alex and I spent the week packing and cleaning. I was happy to end this chapter of my life. I honestly felt like this chapter had gone on a little too long. I was thrilled with my new status in life. I would now be a college graduate. I smiled as I packed up all my stuff in plastic containers and vacuumed the floor of my room. Alex and I spent the rest of that week cleaning our rooms, so on our last day at La Playa, all that we'd have to clean would be the common areas of the apartment. Alex and I had our own separate moving arrangements. Alex rented a U-Haul to move all his stuff to storage until he resumed school. My dad came over to help me move my stuff to his storage area back home. Drew came by to help out, as well. Chan texted Alex, informing him that he would be over to get his remaining items and help out. It was a hot, exhausting summer day. My dad and I moved out my futon, desk, and all my clothes. Alex and Drew moved out Alex's bed and futon.

Once all the big furniture pieces were moved, we all took a break to have lunch.

"Where is Chan?" I asked.

"Mgh, not sure," said Alex, chewing on a sandwich. "He said he would be here," continued Alex.

"His room is still filthy," I said.

"Fuckin' Chan, man!" said Drew, shaking his head as he ate a sandwich.

"His cart-thing is still in the living room," said Alex.

"Not only that, but his chair mat is still in his room, along with a giant luggage bag that's in the closet."

"He just left all his stuff?" asked my dad.

I let out a sigh. "It appears that way."

Alex sent him a text that read, "So, are you going to come over and help us clean and get your stuff?"

Chan responded with, "What stuff?"

We all had a laugh.

"How could he not know that he left his stuff?" asked my dad.

"Fuckin' Chan, man!" answered Drew.

My dad had a chuckle.

Alex responded to Chan by providing him an itemized list of all his crap he'd left. Chan said he didn't want it and that he couldn't make it.

This meant that we had to now throw out all of his stuff and clean up after him. Alex's brother Cody came over to help the cause. I scrubbed and dusted my room, and Alex did the same to his. My dad volunteered "as tribute" and took on the task of cleaning Chan's room. My dad must have felt like Mike Rowe from *Dirty Jobs*. This was, indeed, a dirty one. My dad chose to start by cleaning the dirt spiral on Chan's wall. Cody and Drew worked on cleaning the living room and kitchen. I was enraged that Chan would not come to help. I took pleasure in throwing away his ginormous cart that he parked in the living room and, I repeat, never used.

Unfortunately, time was running out, and it seemed like we wouldn't be able to finish cleaning everything on time. Chan's absence had really thrown a wrench in our day. We had to prioritize our cleaning and left Chan's room for last, if there was any extra time. All the furniture was out, and all the floors had been vacuumed. The kitchen and bathrooms were scrubbed. Alex, Drew, and Cody were working on cleaning out the fridge. I forgot to mention that Chan had left a giant piece of meat and a bunch of chicken frozen in the freezer. Cody and Alex were now tasked with tossing it out. Drew cleaned the plates that had been stacked up in Chan's room for months. #Yuck

I took a break from frantically cleaning to check my phone. "Shit!"

We had twenty minutes until we were supposed to return our keys and be out.

"Hold up," I said, "how are we going to turn in our keys if we don't have Chan's?"

"Shit, he's a fucking idiot," said Alex.

"I'm going to ask Janet down at the leasing office what we should do," I announced.

"Okay," said Alex. "We're going to finish up down here."

"I'll be back. Dad, you good?" I said, yelling up into Chan's loft. He was still up there, trying to get all the dirt and grime off Chan's walls.

"Yeah," he said.

I walked over to ask Janet about the key situation. "Hey, Janet," I said.

"Hi," she replied.

"I have a question. So, today is our last day, and I have all the keys except one of them. Can he drop it off later?" I asked.

"Oh yeah, that's fine. We actually don't need the keys until tomorrow. Just put them in an envelope with the unit number and have them in the drop box by seven o'clock tomorrow," she instructed.

"Okay," I said. Back at the apartment, I relayed the information to Alex, who sent Chan the information about returning his key. Chan said he could swing by later that night to drop it off.

By this time, everyone was exhausted. We were already fifteen minutes past our move-out time. Chan's room was a lost cause. We vacuumed the floors and scrubbed some of the walls, but it just wasn't enough. Chan had really done a number on that room. Hopefully, the deposit would cover the cleaning of the walls and the carpet that he had stained. The only thing left to get rid of was Chan's luggage bag.

"That's a nice bag. Why would he leave that?" asked my dad.

"Don't hurt your head trying to logically assess why Chan does the things he does," I said. "Let's open her up."

I unzipped the luggage bag to find a fucking head—a human head! I'm kidding, but it's not that hard to imagine. It would explain a lot, especially the smell. In the luggage bag, we found a brand-new book on the artwork of the films from Hayao Miyazaki which I gifted to my sister. (Please send the Brother of the Year Award this way.) We also found a Blackberry cell phone, some clothes, and a leather wallet with one Magnum condom inside this unusual go-bag. Cody took the wallet, and the Magnum condom to protect the wallet from getting wet.

"Hey, that is a nice bag," said Drew. "Can I keep it?"

"Yeah, go for it!" I said.

We packed up our cleaning supplies and dropped off our keys. Now, it was up to Chan to drop off his set. I put a letter with Alex's and my keys, indicating that those were ours, and if a set was missing, it belonged to Nick Chan. I said goodbye to the guys. As we pulled away from La Playa for the last time, I felt so relieved to be done with school, La Playa, and especially Chan. As awful as it had been living with Chan in the La Playa, I did have a lot of fun memories there. Most of them were from when Chan was not around. Except for today, when he wasn't around—today of all days. He had left us to clean everything. The worst part was that most of the mess was because of him. No use crying over spilled milk, or in this case, spilled curry. *Whatever, fuck 'im. I'm free. I don't have to see or hear from him again.* That thought brought a large smile to my face. I turned over to my father, who was driving us home.

"Thanks for helping me out, I really appreciate it. Also, thanks for taking on Chan's room. You didn't have to do that," I said.

My father turned to me, smiled, and said, "Fuckin' Chan, man!"

Chapter 26 - Spilled Curry

It was now August. It had been three weeks since we moved out of our apartment. I was living with my sister in a hundred-square-foot apartment. I got a job as an assistant at a law office (clearly, I was putting my degree to use). I was "adulting" at the most basic level, but I was done with school and done with Chan. Or so I thought.

"Just when I thought I was out, they pull me back in." - *The Godfather*

In this instance, "them" being La Playa. I got something called a move-out statement in the mail from La Playa. It was basically an excel sheet explaining how much of our security deposit we would be getting back after the cost of preparing the apartment for the next tenant.

The first line indicated our security deposit, which was $600, and $332 of the $600 would go toward apartment cleaning and final utility fees, leaving $268 to be refunded. *That's a little less than last year*, I thought. Last year, Alex and I had gotten back $400 of our $600 deposit, but last year we hadn't lived with a Tasmanian Devil named Chan. Then, below the "amount refunded" line, there were additional charges for apartment cleaning, carpet cleaning, carpet replacement, and painting. After applying the rest of our deposit, the $268, to the additional charges, we now **owed** $516.38. What the frick! I went online to our apartment portal to get more detail. The fees were broken down into two categories, painting for $89.28 and carpet replacement for $427.10, for a total of $516.38. I began to calculate out what I owed for painting. I had never chipped a wall, and I had scrubbed every wall except for the walls in Chan's room. Carpet replacement? I never spilled anything on the floor. The carpet in my room was spotless. I know it was spotless because I'm a weirdo and bought an area rug to put on top of the already carpeted floor.

Then I thought, *How could Chan not pay for this?* He had stained the floor countless times. He would walk out back without his shoes when he would smoke, tracking dirt into the house and then onto the walls. He had chipped and smudged the walls with his bike. There had been so much blood and dirt on his room walls, it had looked like a set piece from *The Walking Dead*. I quickly forwarded the letter to Alex to see what he thought. He replied with, "Make that dumb fuck pay."

Now I was going to have to be the bad cop. I hate conflict, but this was just ridiculous. I would have been willing to split the cost of clean-up, had I taken the same liberties as Chan, and done my own bloody, dirty wall art installation. I couldn't let Chan go on living in society without notifying him that there are very real consequences to his actions. Despite my anxiety about this inevitable confrontation, I persevered and embraced my David and Goliath moment (not to brag, but

Chan's a little bigger than Goliath, so feel free to call me a hero).

I constructed a text and then sent it to Alex to make sure I had properly addressed the issue and conveyed the right message. Once I got the OK from Alex, my text chain with Chan went like this.

Me: Aug 2nd, 2016, 7:44 p.m.

Hey Chan, so not sure if you were notified by the La Playa, but they sent a letter. You owe $516.38. This fee is for the carpet replacement (remember the curry incident?), painting (bike scuffs and paint chips on the wall), the cleaning of the walls in your room (the blood stains and the dirt marks on the wall next to your desk). You can pay the La Playa via their website Portal. THIS PAYMENT IS DUE THURSDAY! (8/11)

Try to pay by the deadline, the consequences could affect all our credit.

Hope you're having a great summer, and a fun time at Oracle. ☐

P.S. I am not a fan of the latest Pokémon Go update.

Chan: Aug 8th, 2016 7:39 p.m.

Hey, sorry, I have been busy and haven't been able to respond. I understand that some of the responsibility lies on me for the repairs, but I was not the only one who lived there. You and Alex also lived there. You and Alex also made a mess. On top of that, we had to stay and pay rent, even though we did not live at the apartment while you lived there. You told us you would pay for the rent and then welcomed on the deal. I believe the $500 should be split three ways and not have the burden lie on just me. I just Venmo'd the $145 I owed you as well.

Clearly, my attempt to get Chan to realize his fault in the matter ran into a Chan—I mean, wall—actually, same thing.

Me: Aug 9th, 2016 7:40 p.m.

1. Thanks for paying me back for June bills.

2. To address the statement, "You and Alex also made a mess": Any mess I made, I cleaned up. After I moved all my stuff out, I spent time cleaning. I scrubbed the walls and fixtures in my room. I then thoroughly vacuumed the carpet in my room, leaving it looking how it did when I first moved in. After I finished cleaning my room, I then vacuumed the living room. While I vacuumed the living room, my dad cleaned the ledge in your room. As you can see, I didn't just pack up and leave. I generously stayed and cleaned. Unfortunately, I did not have the time nor the energy to clean the walls and floors of your room. So, your floors were dusty, walls dirty and bloody.

3. If you go on to read the bill online, you can see the charges are for paint for the walls and carpet replacement (I'll attach it). The carpet needed to be replaced the moment you spilled curry on it. Curry stains if not cleaned in a timely manner...Just like blood. You also didn't clean the scuff marks on the hallway wall from your bike. Again, I didn't have time to clean up after you.

4. Now to address the statement, "On top of that, we had to stay and pay rent, even though we did not live at the apartment while you lived there. You told us you would pay rent then welcomed on the deal." Maybe you misunderstood what I was suggesting. I would pay rent (the $3400) if you and Alex were inclined to opt out of the lease. We also collectively didn't have the opt-out idea until it was almost too late. Since you and Alex were not proactive about contacting La Playa and opting out, you (and Alex) were on the hook for your portion of rent as stipulated by the lease agreement. Which binds us for 12 months (July 23, 2015-July 23, 2016). Regardless if you find another residence to reside in before the end of the 12-month lease term.

5. So, from my perspective, it seems like you left a mess and now expect Alex and myself to pay the fees for you not cleaning up. So please provide some insight to clarify the situation if I happen to be misreading it. I'm just having a hard time figuring out where I'm at fault.

Chan: Aug 10th, 2016 6:30 a.m.

Alright, look, I never wanted this to be a big deal, and you just pin the blame on me when we all lived there for an extended period of time. I do not think it is fair for me to pay the whole thing by myself. My family paid for the rent for 2 extra months even though I did not live there. I do not know what happened in that period of time while you and Drew lived there. You said you cleaned up, but failed to notify me that there was still a mess, even after leaving. You could have told me there was still a mess, even after leaving, but did not for one reason or another. You are blaming me and Alex for not being proactive when we were relying on you for information. Additionally, I also relied on you to tell me if and when we would together hire cleaners to clean out the apartment. You specifically mentioned that to me. You lived at the apartment when I was busy with life and had the opportunity multiple times to reach out and help me a little bit. It, to me, was a breach of trust. I would have opted to help pay for whatever cleaning service, as we had agreed upon. The blood and curry stains were not the sole reason for the removal of carpet, to me. They did not specify any reason. Please, I do not want this to become an issue, I would love if we just split it instead of having these stupid, passive-aggressive texts over a tribal matter of money, when we all lived together. We are all to blame, and blaming me alone is sort of petty to me.

I also paid utilities, even though I did not live there.

Chan: Aug 10th, 2016 6:30 am

I paid for my third.

Me: Aug 14th, 2016 (Draft)

1 "You just pin the blame on me," Chan, did you clean your floors before you left? Did you scrub the walls before you left? Did you help with any cleaning before you left? Did you spill curry on the carpet and then go to the gym before buying stain remover? Truthfully answer these questions. I'm not just blaming you out of nowhere. There is merit to my accusations. We are being charged with walls and carpet. You didn't clean your walls, and you damaged the carpet.

2. "My family paid for 2 extra months, even though I did not live there." Your family didn't pay 2 "extra" months. They paid for the amount of time agreed upon in the lease agreement (12 months).

3. "You said you cleaned up but failed to notify me that there was still a mess, even after you left." It's not my responsibility to notify you. It should be common sense to clean up after yourself. Alex and I are not your parents; it's not our responsibility to clean up after you.

4. "We were relying on you for information." Again, not my responsibility. You and Alex are both adults. You guys are both capable of using Google. If you wanted to hire cleaners, you should have done it. Again, not my responsibility. I only agreed that getting cleaners was a good idea.

5. "You lived at the apartment when I was busy with life and had the opportunity multiple times to reach out and help me a little bit. It, to me, was a breach of trust." Not sure what the context is for this. But, again, it's not my responsibility to reach out to you.

6. "I would have opted to help pay for whatever cleaning service, as we had agreed upon." Should have been proactive and done it.

7. "The blood and curry stains were not the sole reason for the removal of carpet, to me. They did not specify any reason." We're being charged for the walls and carpet, and both are things you dirtied and did not clean. I mean, they both stain if not cleaned right away. You didn't clean the curry right

away. And the blood wasn't cleaned at all. It's not a coincidence that the charges are for two things you damaged.

8. "Please, I do not this to become an issue, I would love if we just split it instead of having these stupid, passive-aggressive texts over a tribal matter of money, when we all lived together. We are all to blame, and blaming me alone is sort of petty to me." What's petty is never cleaning all year. Then to leave not only a mess but to leave items for your roommates to throw out. Especially when your roommates have cleaned up after you all year.

Here is where your logic is flawed.

"We are all to blame, and blaming me alone is sort of petty"

This statement would be true if Alex and I never cleaned and did not clean before we left. However, we cleaned all the time (at least once a month), mainly after you. And we cleaned before we left. Since you seem oblivious to the concept of cleaning, I'll tell you how it works. So, let's say I make a mess. I clean the mess, making it disappear. When you clean a mess, you don't get charged for the cleaning of said mess. We are not to blame. You are. And you wanting to have Alex and I pay for the cleaning of your mess, that's petty.

After I drafted this retort, I began to question what this would accomplish. What am I doing? I'm trying to argue logically with an illogical person. I began to think about the situation and my experiences with Chan, and I came to the realization that he doesn't see fault on his part because he truly believes he didn't do anything wrong. He has a proclivity for insufferable ignorance, and I suspect, if Chan were to read this book, he would deny every event. Not because he didn't remember them, because for him there was nothing to remember, as if they never happened. He was oblivious to the occurrence of the events, making them non-existent to him. I knew after Chan paid a third of the bill, he wouldn't pay any more. Alex and I paid our thirds and moved on with our lives.

Well, Alex did. I couldn't move past it. I couldn't fathom that Chan was just allowed to roam around freely without a caretaker or some sort of guardian, or at least a leash. I felt like I had to share this story about Chan. Chan and people like him exist. There is a scene at the end of *The Dark Knight* where Alfred tells a story about a jewel thief who steals all sorts of diamonds and rubies, but then the thief dumps the jewels as if they are worthless. Alfred uses this story of the jewel thief as a metaphor for the Joker's motives. He says, "Some people just want to watch the world burn." In Chan's case, he didn't even know he had started the fire. What type of person would I be if didn't speak up about Chan? You know, the whole "if you see something, say something"? I feel it's my civic responsibility to share this story, and warn the world (yes, I know—I'm a hero, a modern-day Paul Revere). The next time you happen to be arguing with a Grade-A moron, consider the possibility that they are a Chan. They deny reality because they are oblivious to it. In which case, save your energy and just let it go. Further interaction is futile. Or, if you are of the grudge-holding variety, you can do what I did and write a snarky book about them.

I can't say this whole Chan experience made me a better person or that I learned much. I just happened to have the misfortune of living with an oblivious moron. It was like living with Michael Scott, turned up to eleven. If you don't know who Michael Scott is, then why the hell are you reading this book? I desperately wish I could say living with Chan made me a more patient and understanding person, but I'm the same. No growth to be had. I went into this thing an asshole and I'm coming out the same way I came in, the asshole. The one good piece of solace I had from this experience was that it was over. I was done with school. I was rid of Chan. I had great memories of hanging out with Ash and trying to flirt with Kimberley. That was it. All I have now are memories. These individuals, who had consumed so much of my life, are now gone forever, like a Snapchat.

If you have made it this far and are still wondering why I wrote this book or what this book is about, this paragraph is for you. Did I write this book out of spite? Sure. If you think this book is a cautionary tale about a crappy roommate, then you have missed the message of this book completely. This book isn't about college, or even Chan, for that matter. It's about bad parenting. It's not an obvious message, I know, but trust me, it's there. You gotta dig deep, real deep. Like Stanley Yelnats, Chan's parents should have prepared him better.

Maybe they couldn't help him because they, too, were unaware of their own Chanisms? They could, perhaps, also be the products of poor parenting. We have to put time and effort into preparing kids for society before sending them off into the world. We, as a people, have to do better, try harder, and invest everything into our kids. They must learn that their actions have consequence that impact themselves and others. It's the third law of physics: for every action, there is an equal and opposite reaction. We can't be content having our children be oblivious morons because, one day, that oblivious moron could go on to be president.

The End

About the Author

Nick Rafter was born and raised in the San Francisco Bay Area, California. Having overcome the obstacles of dyslexia, he garnered a B.A. in Creative Arts from San Jose University. He enjoys his friends, family, and food. As a freshman in high school, he won the first-place award for best fiction story in a local writing contest. The story was about a heavyset cat that learns Kung Fu in a dojo with other animal martial artists. (The film Kung Fu Panda is suspiciously similar.) Nick is cynical, witty, and counter-cultural. These qualities emerge on Instagram where Nick shares his observations. Connect with Nick below.

Email: SpilledCurry@gmail.com

 nickrafter    the_spilled_curry

Acknowledgements

Special thanks to
Alex Banks

Phyllis Voisenat

Marisa Rafter

Dave Rafter

Marianne Ongoco

Drew Fetzer

www.ingramcontent.com/pod-product-compliance
Lightning Source LLC
LaVergne TN
LVHW041540070426
835507LV00011B/839